I0681374

Outrage:
A Protest Anthology For Injustice in a Post 9/11 World

Edited by
Rossy Evelin Lima
&
Christopher Carmona

Slough Press   Kyle~Alamo

Copyright© 2015

All rights reserved

For orders and information:

Slough Press
334 Spring Dr.
Kyle, Texas 78640.

or

Slough Press
939 W. De Soto Ave.
Alamo, TX 78516

Cover Art by Christopher Carmona

Book Design & Cover Art by
Rossy Evelin Lima & Christopher Carmona

ISBN-10: 0941720489   ISBN-13: 978-0-941720-48-9

Library of Congress Control Number: 2015954807

Una nota del editor

La poesía compilada en esta antología secunda el celebre verso de Bécquer, "Mientras haya en el mundo primavera, habrá poesía". Nuestra primavera se fermenta en la sangre sobre la tierra, en el dolor conjunto, anulando continentes y las líneas de aire que cortan y separan. Los versos recopilados provienen de decenas de poetas que no reconocen la primavera de Becker, pero conocen las flores del espíritu descarnado de la madre sin su hijo. No conocen de mistrales, pues les hace falta el aire de nuestro hermano afroamericano en Estados Unidos. No saben del petricor, pero vive el estruendo que quema en las calles de México y Sarajevo y Chicago y Egipto y mi barrio y tu barrio. Nuestra primavera se viste de carmín y no conoce la lira. No calla ni es complaciente. Nos ha hecho germinar los puños como magnolias. Alzar la voz y enraizarnos, vamos siendo una sola enredadera sobre los muros que logran contener nuestros cuerpos mas no nuestras palabras. Esta primavera es diferente, es trascendente porque nos trajo hasta aquí desde los centros de la hermandad que reconocemos. Esta primavera tiene puños, grita, exige, de-sen-mas-cara, protesta y es un solo rostro, esta primavera es nuestra y mientras haya en el mundo primavera, habrá poesía.

-Rossy Evelin Lima

A Note From the Editor

  The inspiration for putting this anthology together came from sitting in a doctor's office, getting an allergy test done, and being forced to sit completely still for twelve minutes while they poked and prodded me. In this office was a TV overhead which was tuned to CNN and on this day, December 4, 2014, the New York City District Attorney's Office announced that it was not going to press charges against the cops that choked Eric Garner to death. It was a watershed moment for me and for the country because once again, on the heels of the Ferguson Riots, police were not being held accountable for another poor man's death, especially since his skin was brown. He died being videotaped and not even that video could get Eric Garner's killer an indictment. So while watching several pundits and "experts" discuss race in America, I thought, what we need now is a people's response. And that response is Outrage! But not through guns, pipes, or fists but with words. I believe that we have not had a proper poetic and artistic response to atrocities around the world in the last couple of years and so this anthology, I hope, offers that. I chose the marker of 9/11 which was the worst terroristic attack on U.S. soil, but it was also the excuse used by the powers that be to terrorize brown people from all over the world under the Red Scare of "terrorism." So, this anthology showcases voices from all over the world talking about injustice and responding in the best way we know how: through words and images for people to remember that we were here, we spoke, and we will speak again because as Audre Lorde once wrote, "Revolution is not a one time event."

-Christopher Carmona

"POETRY IS THE LIFEBLOOD OF REBELLION, REVOLUTION,
AND THE RAISING OF CONSCIOUSNESS."
                                        --ALICE WALKER

Table of Contents

Part IV

A TOAST TO THE POETRY OF PROTEST!
A PROTEST INTRODUCTION

Back around 1992, I walked into the teacher's break room to buy juice from a vending machine before an upcoming class. I had only a few minutes to spare, but found one of my fellow teachers visibly disturbed sitting slumped over a table.

The young teacher lived in the apartment above me, and spent his spare time either skiing in the mountains nearby, or courting women in our town. He was a handsome and confidant gay blade, usually.

I had but minutes to go before my class, but something on the man's face told me I needed to go up to him, sit down, and talk, even if it meant being late or missing entirely my class.

It turned out that my jovial and tall acquaintance was in a total meltdown from a sharp insult some student had thrown at him in his class. I stayed with the man the next half hour talking, occasionally putting my hand on his shoulder, and eventually he came around and got himself together.

I don't remember what I said to him, or what exactly he said to me.

This kind of thing happens every now and then. Students have broken down in my office, men and women. It may be their families, their significant others, or their roommates, that have caused the meltdown without knowing it. Many times I have walked crying college students over to the counseling center on campus. Other times I have let people—grown adults, not students--stay in my home for weeks and months and eat at our table.

Do I get any big thanks for this? Not much. Once and a while -- but I am not looking for thanks -- and I understand how saying thanks can be embarrassing. I don't need thanks. I am glad to help out. I have been told I have a kind face, although I'm not the kindest person, but I am a good listener.

And people have been there for me during my meltdowns. Life works best in a give and take that way.

This may seem an unusual way to approach the topic of protest poetry, but I find it appropriate. I bet you have been in the situation I describe above—unless you are young—and so you know the power of a few words at the right moment to lift people out of a crisis and set them on a path of healing.

Protest poems are most often constructed of a powerful set of beautiful words, and readers seem to find them at the right moment. They are written by those who have faith in the magical power of language to change and heal. Many poets have the idea that we must strive for perfection and immortality in poetry, but no art is perfect or immortal. I learned from the poet Ricardo Sanchez that some poems can be written for a particular unjust situation, and if the poems don't long outlive the rectification of that situation, that's fine. Still, some protest poems last a good long while. I give an example below.

Some might think that protest poems must be angry, and at times anger appears in protest poems directed at a particular injustice, but love rides deeper in these works. The protest poem exists to help people and has a close relationship with readers. A deep love for people and the situation they are in leads poets to attempt, with a few words, to give emotional comfort and assist in overcoming injustice. Poets, thank our lucky stars above, can turn out to be compassionate people, with concerns going far beyond their own personal problems and situations.

I grew up a few blocks from where Carl Sandburg lived in Elmhurst, Illinois. My junior high was named for him and he came to its opening celebration, smoking cigars and putting his boots up on the white table linen—or so the legend goes. Sandburg attended Knox College, where one of the Lincoln/Douglas debates occurred, and his first book of poems was published by a professor's small press there in Galesburg, Illinois.

Here is a protest prose poem by Carl Sandburg. You will no doubt see some irony and satire, but you will feel affection and admiration for the men he is concerned about. Protest poems are a great reach of love because the poet is forgetting herself -- or himself -- and speaking out about a situation that has painful, unjust influence on many people's daily lives.

The Mayor of Gary

I asked the mayor of Gary about the 12-hour day and the 7-day week. And the mayor of Gary answered more workmen steal time on the job in Gary than any other place in the United States. "Go into the plants and you will see men sitting around doing nothing--machinery does everything," said the mayor of Gary when I asked him about the 12-hour day and the 7-day week. And he wore cool cream pants, the Mayor of Gary, and white shoes, and a barber had fixed him up with

a shampoo and a shave and he was easy and imperturbable
though the government weather bureau thermometer said 96
and children were soaking their heads at bubbling fountains
on the street corners.   And I said good-bye to the Mayor of
Gary and I went out from the city hall and turned the corner
into Broadway.   And I saw workmen wearing leather shoes
scuffed with fire and cinders, and pitted with little holes from
running molten steel,   And some had bunches of specialized
muscles around their shoulder blades hard as pig iron,
muscles of their forearms were sheet steel and they looked to
me like men who had been somewhere.

[GARY, INDIANNA, 1915]

Gary, Indiana is a steel-making city, with Bessemer furnaces
flaring brightly through the night, just over the state line from
Chicago. Needless to say, we now have a forty-hour workweek,
although that workweek is under threat. This protest poem did its job.
Many such protest poems and protests are what brought about the
change. Protest poems may need to go to work again in the future to
protect this workers' right.

You may see in certain circles an outright hostility toward
protest poems. I was told in graduate school that I could not write a
dissertation about the protest poetry of World War I. I desperately
needed to write that dissertation because it was protest poems
by writers like Wilfred Owens, particularly his sonnet "Dulce Et
Decorum Est," that kept me sane during the Vietnam War. Only in a
poem could I find comfort and confirmation that I was not crazy for
being anti-war. All the powerful media and leaders of the nation at
the time were calling me a crazy, shiftless bum.

Obviously some poets and people are going to be happy with the
way things are going in their part of the world. The world is full
of all kinds of people and poets. If some artists are not inspired or
drawn to protest the way things are, I don't necessarily hold it against
them. Perhaps it is not in their natures, or perhaps they have led
lucky lives. Tess Gallagher said something to the effect, 'Poetry is a
mansion with many rooms.' I wish she had said that poetry is a house
with many rooms, because poetry serves as the preferred medium
for the marginalized and poor as an inexpensive art. All you need
is a photocopy machine and a stapler to produce multiple books of
poetry. Poetry can take the risks and say things first because it does
not depend on wealthy producers, as theatre, dance, movies, TV,

opera and even rock concerts these days seem to require. The poet does not have to play it safe; the poet is not worried about the loss of large sums of money.

But don't let it get you down if some remain hostile toward your drive to protest in poems. Don't let yourself be beaten down so that you shut up, although I must admit at times people have gotten me to shut up. They have typecast me as nothing more than a protest poet, or they have dismissed my work because they thought all I did was protest and to protest was to write poorly. The truth is I never wrote enough protest poems. Making and living and caring for children took up most of my life, and, also, much of the time I was not experiencing directly any terrible injustice.

Yet, if you are a person with compassion and love, a person concerned with how things are going for people, for animals, and even for plants, then you may have in you the need to speak out in protest poems, to be a voice for those without a voice. In the twentieth and twenty-first centuries we have had wonderful protest poetry concerned about wars, about the environment, about gay rights, and about Asian, black, and brown civil rights. Many poets you know may have participated in demonstrations. Some you are reading these words here may have been pushed and shoved, chained and locked up in jail. Good for you if you protested an unjust law or practice! It may or may not have accomplished the goal immediately, but with right on your side a strong chance exists right will win in the long run.

Poets are not flowers. They're like the tough desert ocotillo, and no more suicidal than those in business. Poets seek to change and heal with words. To be a tough poet it also helps if you have nearby a group of simpatico poets who share your desire to try to make this world a better place.

A poet needs a community of like-minded artists because, not surprisingly, when you protest there will be "push back." Mostly what I've experienced are anti-Semitic letters full of vicious and violent words and drawings, even though I am not Jewish. I was fortunate to know well and be inspired over the years by Raul Salinas and Ricardo Sanchez—poets who were not afraid to speak out about injustices— and also inspired by correspondence with the poets Gary Snyder and Antler. When the Chicago black author Gwendolyn Brooks got involved in the civil rights movement in the 1960's, she dropped her connection with large New York City prestige presses and turned to the African-American small presses of her community.

Consider the poets in this anthology your community. Get in

contact with them through the publisher of this book, dear readers and writers, if they hit on an injustice crucial to you by their words. Remember, protest poems are a way of standing up to the many types of bullies in the world. We have bullies amongst the good kids in schools, and we have bully cops amongst the good cops on the beat. Bully cops can be more dangerous than bully kids so we must use the awesome power of weightless, invisible words to embarrass them, to get them off the police force or into retraining (depending on the situation), and to help bring about change so other cities don't explode like Ferguson, Missouri.

A protest poem is a small, seemingly insignificant stone thrown in a pond whose energy radiates and ripples out in all directions to reach the whole wide world of shore. Protest poems possess mysterious, miraculous power. An entire state, like Arizona, can eliminate a large educational program, due to the influence of one ignorant but powerful man, but because the poets and artists protest, clandestine libraries have bloomed all through the amazing Arizona desert landscape to provide the material taken out of schools.

Many kinds of protest poems can be written, so perhaps even the bullies with billions of bucks will find flowers blooming all over their skin. Protest poems can be funny, satiric, ironic, direct, or indirect. They can also be poems of witness that point to and show injustice, as Whitman seems to do so eloquently in his poem "The Wound Dresser." The poet paints a picture in words. Billy Holiday sang a poem about lynching that does not use the word. It is called "Strange Fruit" and was written by teacher and songwriter Abel Meeropol. Billy shocked her Yankee audiences, but her 'poem-turned-song' brought awareness to this horrid yet widespread practice and helped bring change.

So what are you waiting for, reader? Read these poems to find out and be inflamed by what's gone wrong in the world. Share them with those you know and love, and then write your own protest poems, to be printed and read at readings in your hometown and in the world. Get busy and give service. It will make your life more meaningful.

It's the grass roots way to spread powerful, magical words of concern and caring and to help bring about change. You do not do it to make money. You do it out of love.

-Chuck Taylor

Part I

"THE REVOLUTION IS NOT AN APPLE THAT FALLS WHEN IT IS
RIPE. YOU HAVE TO MAKE IT FALL."
-CHE GUEVARA

Claudia Hernández

<u>Poetas contra la mala educación</u>

Vimeesh Maniyur

Don't be our fathers

We are not your children
We don't know you even as strangers
Then who are you to take our patent?
Don't be our fathers.

We have one in our homes
Many in our bloods
And many more to live with
They are the ones
Who always want us to be with them
Look, they don't want any title to love
Don't be our fathers

We don't want any children to be their fathers
We are fathers of our own children
And children of our own fathers
So don't be our fathers.

Every...

Every war is a trick
To ensure
The innocent dead.
 Every war is a kick
To shut
The dreaming voice.
Every dead is a walk
To ensure
The innocent rise
Every dead is a dream
To kick
The Living innocent

Abraham Peralta Vélez

Mineral de angustia

Como un mineral de angustia,
como el azufre dorado,
podía salir al volcán de labores,
deambular alrededor de una taza de café,
caminar bajo la lluvia del hambre,
y aguantarme, atribulado,
las ganas de romperme
    en un desastroso llanto.
Podía
incluso
amar
y reír
en el redondel de los besos. Pero
una úlcera de sombra reclamaba el desastre.
Era una enfermedad de toro.
Era porque se vivía en ruedo.

Era necesario ser piedra,
mineral inorgánico, beligerante,
para soportar ver a un hermano colérico
gritando de locura
                en medio del volcán
 del miedo,
para ver a un viejo a punto de morir
 en el colmillo de la calle
para ver lo que hay que ver
en esta nauseabunda ciudad líquida.

Y no hacer nada.
Era necesario y era terrible serlo
y seguir
y no poder ser la flama deseada
mientras, se busca en las orillas
del alumbrado
dónde los gorriones anidan
su vatios de esperanza.

3

Tragafuegos

-ensayo poema-
Yo miro la noche a través de los barrotes
y, a pesar de todos estos muros que me oprimen el pecho,
mi corazón palpita con la estrella más lejana.
              -Nazim Hikmet, "Angina de pecho", Poemas desde la cárcel

Nada en el mundo cambia por este poema.
Este poema no es una gran noticia.
Es tan minúsculo como lo invisible vital.
O quizá menos...
No sirve este papel para cruzar una frontera.
No sirve para conseguir un buen trabajo.
Ni vale más que una moneda.
El poema no es moneda de cambio.
¿Para qué sirve esta insistencia?
Nada en el mundo cambia por este poema.
Continuarán los tragafuegos
-cada uno de nosotros-
incendiando las calles.
Y habrá quienes seguirán creyendo
que pueden jugar a los dados
con el mineral de la tierra
con el mineral de las hombres
y con la sal de los mares
hasta colmar de ceniza la primavera.

Nada en el mundo cambia por este poema.
La rosa roja en su jardín mohíno
seguirá cavando
su propia tumba de sangre.
Seguirá un muerto tras otro
    desollado
a la orilla de la carretera
y saldrá en un periódico más
como si cayera la manecilla del segundero.

Nada cambia, pero sí alguien.
Porque algo es cierto
-si me has seguido hasta aquí-

que de alguna forma
te está siendo útil este poema
como quien besa el vientre de una embarazada
y siente
y siente
y siente
que quiere cruzar la víspera de su miseria
porque está amando hasta el colmo de la inocencia
el amor porvenir en el vientre de su amada.

Isaac Chavarría

ode to border patrol agent blanco
                    Falfurrias, TX

brash and determined
leaning on my driver side door
i become enamored, yet frightened

you ask

is this your wife?
today, she's still just a lover

how long have you been together?
as long as a secret can last

all details family and friends
avoid and shun

maybe you genuinely care
but twice i'm asked, is this your car?
i try to sound sincere when saying yes, sir.

worse, you ask about my employment
pan am, the university
and i'm afraid to say my job isn't secure

i am insecure
are your german shepherds trained
on the scent of marijuana or fear?

do you have an ethno fetish
and single out bronze tones?

if i admit i am a pocho, will you reject me too?

you let us pass into the second part
of the united states

on our return
nearing the border patrol station
i smile for 10 instant cameras
hoping you'll see

i'm the one
catching you in the rearview
periquiando con otros

Ode to KRGV News Channel 5

Headline: Number of Illegal Crossers Declining

Illegal Aliens
Illegal Crossers
Illegal Floods
Illegal Marriage
Illegal Swarm of Bees
Illegal Grazing
Illegal Tax Subsidies
Illegal Drowning
Illegal Hamburger, Hot Dog Buns
Illegal Chase
Illegal Grant Schemes
Illegal Disaster
Illegal Dumping
Illegal Sewage Seeping
Illegal SpaceX
Illegal Health Services
Illegal Mass
Illegal Education
Illegal Life

Me'ira Pitkapaasi

Good Intentions

It started out with good intentions. My brown child had been having panic attacks about leaving our apartment and being "shot by a white cop." He refused to go to school for over a week. Following trusted advice, I contacted a local police department and asked them if they would be willing to have a white and non-white police officer meet with my eleven-year-old. My hope was that they would show him that police officers were the good guys, not violent racists as we had been seeing and hearing about every day recently.

We were met by the chief of the department, a white-haired white-skinned man who welcomed us with open arms. He took us up to his office, gave us his personalized baseball card, a bunch of police coloring books, and deputized my little boy as an honorary police officer, badge and all. He introduced us to several officers and administrators- all white. He asked them to take us to various areas of the police station, introduce us to the various officers and detectives- all white.

But still, it seemed to be working. My young man of color was feeling less and less anxious, even starting to smile and speak with the various individuals who were being so kind to and gentle with him. They told us about the neighborhood program they did with all of the fifth grade classes in the local school district, and that they were planning on being in my son's classroom one day this week.

Convinced that all was well, that my son was going to find a way to go about his daily life again without the terror of being shot by a white police officer that had plagued him for weeks on end, we walked out with an officer who had made an especially close bond with my son. He showed us his police car, even turned on the blinking lights for him, showed him the laptop that was built into his dashboard, and let him have a peek inside the back of the car, where he kept the "bad guys."

And as we walked through the chilly air to our car, the officer told me more about the fifth grade class neighborhood program, and how it had gotten its beginnings. Apparently there had been a certain class of fifth graders that had already been giving them trouble. The department wanted to go in, make their presence known, and begin to establish a positive relationship with these children.

I thought the events in Ferguson, the loss of Michael Brown, the decision of the Grand Jury, the loss of Eric Garner, Rumain Brisbon, Tamir Rice- the same age as my little boy- I thought they had opened my eyes. Holding my small brown son tightly while he cried hysterically in fear of police men and other white men in his life- I thought these experiences had truly made me see the depth of the institutionalized racism still alive and rampant in our country today.

And then this kind police officer who had so sweetly calmed the fears of my child, he told me the name of the elementary school where the program had started. When the school's name didn't register with me, he clarified… "You know- the one where all the black kids go."

Carlos Aguasaco

<u>Los nombres de Juárez</u>

[Poema compuesto con la lista real de los nombres de las víctimas de feminicidio reciente en ciudad Juárez, México.]

¿Qué sabes de Adriana, Aída, Alejandra, Alicia, Alma, Amalia, Amelia o Amparo? ¿Qué sabes de Ana, Apolonia, Araceli, Aracely con i griega o Bárbara? ¿Qué sabes de Bertha, Blanca, Brenda, Brisa, Carolina, Cecilia, Celia, Cynthia, Clara, Claudia o Dalia? ¿Qué sabes de Deisy, Domitila, Donna, Dora, Elba, Elena o Elsa? ¿Qué sabes de ellas, de alguna de ellas o de Elizabeth, Elodia, Elva con uve, Elvira, Emilia o Eréndida? ¿Qué sabes de ellas, de alguna de ellas, de sus muertes, de sus últimas palabras o de Erica, Erika con Ka, Esmeralda, Estefanía, Eugenia, Fabiola, Fátima, Flor o Francisca? ¿Qué sabes de ellas, de alguna de ellas, de sus muertes, de sus últimas palabras, de sus llamados de auxilio, del hilo de sangre con que llevaban el alma atada al cuerpo o de Gabriela, Gladys, Gloria, Graciela, Guadalupe, Guillermina, Hester con su hache invisible en el aire o de Hilda? ¿Qué sabes de ellas, de alguna de ellas, de sus sueños, de sus recuerdos, de su recuerdo, de sus lápidas o de Ignacia, Inés, Irene, Irma, Jacqueline, Jessica con doble ese y sin acento, Juana, Julia o Julieta? ¿Qué sabes de ellas, que cualquiera de ellas, de los ojos que lloran su ausencia o de Karina, Laura, Leticia, Lilia, Liliana, Linda, Lorenza, Lourdes, Luz o Manuela? ¿Qué sabes de ellas, de la más joven de ellas, de sus manos juntas como en oración buscando la paz de la justicia o de Marcela, Margarita, María, María, María, María, cuarenta veces María? ¿Qué sabes de ellas, de alguna de ellas, de sus memorias, de sus sonrisas acalladas con violencia o de Maribel, Maritza, Martha, Mayra, Merced, Mireya, Miriam o Nancy? ¿Qué sabes de ellas, de la más baja de ellas, de sus zapatos con lodo, de su relicario de plata, de su mano entre abierta y levantada como para saludarte o de Nelly, Nora, Norma, Olga, Otilia o Paloma? ¿Qué sabes de ellas, de todas ellas, de la primera de ellas, de su sombra en la tierra, de su corazón roto tres veces y a la vez treces veces zurcido con llanto o de Patricia, Paula, Paulina, Perla, Petra o Raquel? ¿Qué sabes de ellas, de la segunda de ellas, de sus primeros pasos, de sus muñecas, de su espejo de azogue o de Reina, Rocío, Rosa, Rosa como

11

en un coro de Rosas, Rosalba, Rosario o Sandra? ¿Qué sabes de ellas, de la más vieja de ellas, de sus primeras letras, de sus gastos, de sus deudas o de Silvia, Silvia y Silvia, Sofía, Soledad, Sonia, Susana o Teodora? ¿Qué sabes de ellas, de la más alta de ellas, de sus tortillas, sus tacos, de su mole, de sus chiles rellenos o de Teresa, Teresita, Tomasa o Vanesa? ¿Qué sabes de ellas, de la más solitaria de ellas, de su talismán, de su tatuaje, de su marca de nacimiento, de la cicatriz de un parto o de Verónica, Verónica la otra, la otra Verónica que no es Verónica, Victoria, Violeta, Virginia, Viridiana o Yésica? ¿Qué sabes de ellas, de la más alegre de ellas, de sus canciones, de sus polleras, de su cumpleaños, del día de su santo, de sus mañanitas o de Yolanda, Yolanda, Zenaida o Zulema? ¿Qué sabes de ellas –dime-, de todas ellas, de cualquiera de ellas, de sus dolientes, de sus amigos, de sus hermanos, de sus hijos, de su bautismo, de sus nombres o de la mujer sin nombre que ha muerto más de setenta veces, de la mujer sin nombre que -¡ay! ¡ay! ¡ay! ¡ay! ¡ay! ¡Dios mío!- sigue muriendo en Juárez sin que nadie haga o diga nada?

Ogunsina Temi-tope

'No skin'

Slavery chapter has keep the bucket
Why skin colour is a crime?
When we quoted "Says No To Racism'
Blacks is not a colour but attitude
'Where is the love' like Black Eye pea
When you sent your brother an errand
Without returning back..........
Oh my goodness! Its painful
Like the lost of M.L.K and Maya Angelou
Don't keep the truth secret
Black is not guity
Black community heart is saying
Stop the killing of blacks
Like the stop of killing of twins
Black is not darkness
Gets the picture clearly
Judge through mind not skin
So, kill the hatred against black
Black is but kindness
Black is but love
And love is but peace
So, like India Arie, looks each other eyes
See no skin but family

'Change

Sleep is the cousin to death like Nas
Wake up everybody like Legend and Common
We are all missionaries
This age is an age of revolutionary
Like Comrade Kim I'll Sung
Pick u the mission of change
Like Ignacio Allende and Miguel Hidalgo
And start the change, you wish to see
In this beautiful society
Because we are all masters of revolution
But revolution is mind
Have the mind of Patrice Lumumba
Don't mind that fear
Silence injustice because injustice is a threat to society
So, become anti-violence like Grandhi
Be like Ken Sarowiwa in society
Use love to make peace like Martin Lurther King
Because revolution is love
So, take love language
To the middle east
And put them in ocean of love
Because love is peace
Only love can give birth to change
So, start loving because society needs change
Revolution is change.

Edna Ochoa

Ompohualli ihuan yei nikanpan (Cuarenta y tres siempre aquí)

Los desaparecidos nos aparecieron. Nos juntaron
No estamos solos, ya nos unimos
Desenterramos la voz de tantos muertos que nos dieron
Y la resurrección viene con nombre de justicia
Nuestros muertos nos han levantado
Nuestros muertos nos empujan a luchar por la vida
¡Vivos los queremos! ¡Vivos nos queremos! ¡Vivos!

Cuarenta y tres suena Cuarenta y tres retumba
Cuarenta y tres nuestras gargantas
Cuarenta y tres nuestros corazones
Cuarenta y tres nos alzan Cuarenta y tres nos hacen llorar
Cuarenta y tres nos limpian las lágrimas
Cuarenta y tres nos detienen el dolor
Y lo levantan a caminar a exigir justicia
Cuarenta y tres nos hacen padres y madres
Estudiantes nos vuelven Cuarenta y tres qué México somos
Cuarenta y tres nos miran con sus ojos extraviados
De no saber por qué ¿Por qué? ¿Por qué?
Cuarenta y tres nos alientan
Cuarenta y tres nos dan rostro
Cuarenta y tres palabra nos dan
Cuarenta y tres fuerza Cuarenta y tres luz
cuarenta y tres memoria abierta Nunca olvido
Cuarenta y tres lucha Cuarenta y tres no detenerse
Cuarenta y tres caracol
Cuarenta y tres Señor y Señora Movimiento
Cuarenta y tres nos han despertado
Cuarenta y tres cataclismo cambio
Cuarenta y tres nos desentierran de los hoyos del olvido

Nos dan su sangre en las moléculas del aire
Su voz joven de hijos de campesinos y maestros
Su voz de tierra natal

Cuarenta y tres patria
Cuarenta y tres raíces semillas, tierra, todo es nuestro

Cuarenta y tres danza Cuarenta y tres canto
Cuarenta y tres jade Cuarenta y tres colibríes Cuarenta y tres minas
Cuarenta y tres mares
Cuarenta y tres nuestras especies de maíz cuarenta y tres nuestros
lugares sagrados
Cuarenta y tres nuestra lenguas
Nuestras costumbres de figura Quetzalcóatl
Cuarenta y tres nuestros recursos
Cuarenta y tres trabajo Cuarenta y tres educación
Cuarenta y tres comunidad Cuarenta y tres arte
Cuarenta y tres ciencia Porvenir
Cuarenta y tres acción y palabra adelantándonos
Cuarenta y tres pueblo resurgido
Cuarenta y tres ternura
Cuarenta y tres resistencia
Cuarenta y tres espiritualidad todo rostro todo vida.

Lynn White

Pictures of Kitties

Look at all the people marching and waving,
waving pencils and pictures of pencils.
Millions and millions marching with pencils,
asserting their values, showing their power
and paying their respects to the drawers.

But it's not what it seems.
say the sideline snipers,
the underminers,
the false flag wavers,
the pencil baiters,
Je Suis Fuck All-ers.

They're pencilled pawns,
just part of the plans
of the Old Pretenders,
the liars and haters,
the manipulators,
the plotters and schemers,
the money makers.
The bullets were blanks and,
the dead, if dead, not heroes.
Say the sideline snipers,
the underminers, the false flag wavers,
the pencil baiters,
Je Suis Fuck All-ers.

Look who's leading from the front line.
It's the Old Pretenders, the liars and haters,
standing together to protect each other.
Proof enough? What more do you need.
But it's not what it seems.
It's a trick of the camera, another pretense
to diminish the distance between them and us,
between them and the leaders behind them
the pencil wavers,
the movers and shakers,

17

the history makers.
Not so say the snipers,
the underminers,
know better than you-ers,
Je Suis Fuck All-ers.

They say nothing of Gaza, those pencil wavers,
or climate, or oil, or this, that, or those.
And if they can't speak for all things,
then they are speaking for nothing,
so it won't matter if, tired by the baiters
they go home and draw cats
till their pencils are blunt
and all is back to where it was
with a bit more hate around.

But look at the smiles
from the Old Pretenders,
the liars and haters,
the leadership fakers,
Je Suis Fuck All-ers
who love
to look at
pictures
of kitties.

Eduardo Quintero

Home

The Game

The Real Borderwall

Javier Gutiérrez Lozano

LET THE APPLAUSE BEGIN

For Diana, Tara and Milan

It had to be said to the world
that in Yugoslavia
we weren't ourselves,
      we were everybody.

Because the path always has two directions
and it cannot be stopped by time,
the direction is created with our footsteps:
there will always be a beginning in the distance
if the stride grasps itself to a constant rhythm.

Perhaps the cell doors are never a place for the guilty,
nonetheless the days of hate will slide off in clean time,
for the hands that could give death,
      are the paint that sprouts in the future.

I hope for all of this to be a theatre spectacle
in which we are everybody, and not a blood, a race,
a humanity destined to break every chain.

Luckily, our hands also
mounted this play
in which we still remain together.

Let the dialogues of our scene,
be those which make everyone return
to the place where we would all be ourselves.

In 1983, Kemal Zuko, resident in the city of Sarajevo, had cerebral
tumor surgery. In spite of being a successful surgery, the ravages
from the tumor were severe and he could never take care of himself.

Kemal spent ten years under his sister's care, who in an international
television interview confessed that when the bombings flared up, she
did not have the strength to stay inside the apartment, abandoning
Kemal to visit him only in the mornings.

Kemal, destined to spend his days in bed, mentioned in front of the TV cameras that nothing scared him, but hunger. Nevertheless, he stood to his word stating that in spite of this enormous tragedy, everything would be fine... everything would be fine (biće bolje...biće bolje).

BIĆE BOLJE

> "In this war nothing hurts anymore
> except hunger."
> -Kemal Zuko

What could be said to the man who has lost everything
if night is the light on his window
and he remembers an unlived life.

Step now, the shore of a river
that was nostalgia, that was the naked body
of a lover,
is now the first step of the fall,
the death that returns with the waters, and the river
a shipyard of one that has forgotten to follow their own steps.

How could I talk about my land, the tree that is my father,
and the deepness of those eyes that awaken me,
that are the origin, the beginning of the blinding riverbed,
when the stream it knows only cleans
the trail of all who have fallen.

How could I talk about you, to this man that believes
winter are the footsteps of someone who departs,
and the snow is the water that avoids the thirsty.

Who am I, my darling, who am I
this whom you love so much,
if not another witness of the disgrace.

What is love, this longing to live in spite of everything.

Def is the man
who answers the voices of the past,
        And I
want to live all that was severed in their lives.

Nothing scares me now
for I have become deaf.
I don't hear the bombings;
I've been deafened by it all…
Biće bolje, biće bolje.

Raúl Sánchez

Under My Breath

My tongue and breath
spout out angry words
distant accounts
close to my skin

closer than what was once lived.
Baton sticks smashing young bodies
cracking bones, blood splattered
on side walk asphalt hard sound

when the bodies fell
protesting, screaming and yelling
demanding justice
aloud for all to hear

rage and injustice cannot be ignored—
new generations awakening
all over the world
Mexico, Ukraine, Palestine, Ferguson, New York.

Some of us can still hear the batons
hitting the pavement
grenadier, military trained cops
shielded dogs behind helmets,

masks hiding their hate vile for the ideals.
Those of us who have stood up for Justice
know the feeling of those moments
we Protested, we protest!

We write, we sing
we bring it out to the people, our people
of all skin colors, languages, ideologies
because injustice is unjust in any language

Bajo mi aliento

De mi aliento y lengua
emanan palabras furiosas
acontecimientos distantes
que lo siento en la piel

más cerca de lo que he experimentado.
Macanas golpeando cuerpos de jóvenes
quebrando huesos, sangre salpicada
en la banqueta, el sonido hueco

de los cuerpos al caer
protestando, gritando vociferantemente
exigiendo justicia
en voz alta para que todos lo oigan

el descontento y la injusticia no pueden ser ignorados—
las nuevas generaciones despiertan
por todo el mundo
México, Ucrania, Palestina, Ferguson, Nueva York.

Algunos de nosotros todavía podemos escuchar las macanas
golpeando el pavimento
granaderos, policías militares entrenados
perros escudados detrás de sus cascos,

máscaras que ocultan su vil odio por los ideales.
Entre nosotros hay algunos que nos hemos manifestado por la
justicia
sabemos lo que se siente en esos momentos
nosotros protestamos, seguimos protestando!

Escribimos, cantamos
lo llevamos a la gente, nuestra gente
de piel de todos colores, idiomas e ideologías
porque la injusticia es injusta en cualquier idioma

Democracy Without Democracy

Democracy is not always democratic
political criticism destroys liberty.
our freedom is not free
every day and every night

someone is always spying on us.
Our texts are stored
our emails read
our photos kidnapped.

The racist cop is not looking for us
but he always finds us—
our skin color makes us visible
whereas light skin folks

don't get bothered.
They look at us as if we—
were from a different planet.
They turn their backs

when they don't understand
our twisted words
they look down
when our last name is García

Hernández or Zapata.
They think we are subversive
cheaters and thieves.
Ignorant people

are just ignorant—
cultureless
uneducated.
We belong

to this ancient land.
Our history carved in stones
only us can tell
with pride, courage, respect.

We know we belong to the elements.
The sun gives us life
the earth, sustenance the rain
heaven's blessing
the moon our shelter
our heart the strength to survive,
we are warriors, Mexicatiahui!

Democracia sin democracia

La democracia no siempre es democrática
la crítica política destruye la libertad
nuestra libertad no es gratuita
todos los días todas las noches

alguien siempre nos está espiando
nuestros textos son almacenados
nuestros e-mails son leídos
nuestras fotos secuestradas

la policía racista no nos busca
pero siempre nos encuentra
el color de nuestra piel nos delata
mientras que a la gente de tez blanca

nadie la toca.
Nos miran como si fuéramos de otro planeta
nos dan la espalda cuando no entienden
nuestras palabras torcidas

cuando nuestro apellido es García
Hernández o Zapata
creen que somos subversivos
engañadores y rateros.

La gente ignorante es simplemente ignorante—
sin cultura ni educación.
Nosotros pertenecemos
a esta tierra ancestral.

Nuestra historia tallada en piedras
sólo nosotros podemos contarla
con orgullo, coraje y respeto.
Sabemos que pertenecemos

a los elementos
el sol nos da vida
la tierra sustento
la lluvia, bendición de los cielos

la luna nuestro refugio
en nuestro corazón
la fuerza para sobrevivir
somos guerreros, Mexicatiahui!

Susan Beall Summers

Running

His mother heard the news
and began running to him
it was too far
and too late
a friend stopped her,
put her in a car and
together they drove
to the police tape
around the scene
of her dead son in a pool of his own blood.
A Grand Jury found no evidence
of wrongdoing by the officer who killed him,
and his mother is sentenced to running
to save her boy
in terror, every night,
always too late.

Mariano Morales

<u>Suerte que hayamos perdido todo</u>

Hace ya tiempo que pasaron los carnavales,
la policía con sus perros,
la Guerra Civil, el Segundo imperio francés.
Pasó el circo con sus elefantes tristes
se acabó el holocausto
se murió el Ché.

Los gritos de libertado también pasaron,
inaudibles, casi desapercibidas,
un aullido un llanto un cantar de voces
que a mi parecer
se parecen a la voz de mi madre.

Hace tiempo ya que se fueron los faisanes,
que volaron lejos en mi dirección,
compraron el Excélsior,
abandonaron la plaza de Mayo,
cerró la isla
y se abrieron 90 millas.

Las luces siempre languidecen,
después de Franco, de Fidel
de Bolivia, de Phnom Penh,
¿quién nos avisó
que donde hace falta
la paz se terminó?

La tierra se hizo vieja
el agua cae del cielo casi por cosumbre
los mangos saben a miel
la carne se volvió un lujo,
el animal un medio,
la television una silla rota,
y la gente un mar de llanto vivo y sordo.

Pasó la Guerra fría,
el dólar subió y se erigieron muros

por hombres
para hombres.

Hace tiempo que la democracia es casi pan,
piedra de iglesia que me hunde,
prostituta de mala caña.

Pasó una mujer
que nos salvó a todos
y nadie nos avisó.

Ay hermano,
cómo pasa el tiempo me dijiste,
fíjate nadamás,
que pasó el tren
la segunda guerra mundial
que pasó el Atleti a la final.
suerte que hayamos perdido todo

Suerte
que hayamos perdido todo.

Kushal Poddar

Those Unsent Messages from A War Zone

From the rubbles and ruins
we gather the smoke rings
of an unsent signal.

Its almost sender
tried to remember
his wife, safe in her grave,
six years below. He failed.

The sky wore that
after blaze darkness,
murky and clear.
A dog whined away,
became a constellation.

Someone says, we should
force a memorial
on the city. I close
my eyes. A smokey star
appears, inhales time.

A dog still wants to sniff
earth and flesh. A man
wants to say, forgetting
is a way to process
memories.

Post Apocalypse

At first it sounds like
a comedians routine-
fire climbs on board, hits
two tall turrets, spawns
its legacy now
seen in markets, huts,
subways-

but one day
I wake up with half
of my hand skinned, burnt.

One day I find my
shadow in a coal-corsage.
Inside a red speck
flickers on and on.

I corrode into your
bone bare structure
with a single kiss.

Sometimes I cannot
stare at the mirror
and unsee a childhood
memory of far away
fiery rings changing peaks.

I hear a plane above,
a burning stag streaming
to the place I stand
and I do not.

Iliana Hernández Partida

<u>País de hojas secas</u>

Mi país es un puñado de hojas secas que se acumulan en cuevas y laberintos donde viven los muertos que no existen en los registros oficiales, por las mañanas tomamos café y pensamos en ellos con un nudo de lágrimas en la garganta que se ha formado con los años, hemos aprendido a sufrir hacia adentro, a creer que toda infamia es posible en el presente.

El día se vive entre las prisas; uno va a trabajar, fluye con el tráfico y su frialdad, se llega al trabajo con cierta sensación de que nunca nos hemos ido de esa rutina, mientras secuencias rápidas de la infancia llegan frente a nuestros ojos, correr con los amigos y los perros en una calle ancha hasta el anochecer, cuando los padres no temían que sus hijos no regresaran enteros al hogar.

La maldad y la burla nos han hecho su presa, asistimos como conejos asustados a las carnicerías que nuestros verdugos celebran en plena luz del día, mujeres que no vuelven de sus trabajos, jóvenes secuestrados, niños que fallecen en guarderías públicas. No hemos olvidado nada ni lo haremos, aunque nos bombardeen con su política pornográfica, sus ademanes de falsos profetas de una nueva patria. De noche vuelan sobre los techos pensamientos dolorosos, me duele tener una cama, cobijas tibias y estas paredes mientras otros son torturados, mi rostro se entumeció cuando los periódicos y los noticieros pregonaron la tragedia que ha sacudido al mundo y puesto a México en el ojo de un huracán que tiene mucho tiempo envolviéndonos a todos, destruyendo familias, arrancando las raíces de nuestra serena alegría, de la tranquilidad que los ciudadanos soñamos tener un día pero que ahora sabemos que era una ilusión. Cuando la oscuridad cae sobre mi habitación busco a tientas mi reloj, son las dos de la mañana y siguen desapareciendo más personas, ¿cuántos cuerpos sin vida encontrarán mañana como si no hubiera importado nada su historia, sus palabras, el país que eran ellos también?

La noche se ha quedado sin estrellas en mi país.

Dormito a ratos buscando alguna luna imposible que ilumine el camino de los estudiantes de Ayotzinapa, todavía hoy 20 de enero de 2015 no hay respuesta ni sabemos qué sucedió con ellos, no aparecen vivos ni han regresado de su tumba para señalar a sus captores o a sus asesinos.

Para el gobierno son el asunto que no debió trascender, la incomodidad, la vergüenza de los pecados que han sido descubiertos

36

ante las demás naciones, para nosotros es el dolor y la pesadilla; es no regresar a ese estado de inocencia que tuvimos, hemos perdido la confianza.

Pienso en Julio César Mondragón y me duele el pecho. Él fue el primero de los estudiantes de Ayotzinapa que cayó bajo las manos de las bestias, pudo escaparse del grupo de estudiantes cuando fueron capturados y huyó entre los arbustos, pensando en salvarse y regresar con su esposa y su pequeña hija. Pero fue alcanzado por las garras y lo humillaron, nos escupieron como a él, le arrancaron el rostro y nos lo arrancaron a nosotros, a todos los mexicanos, lo torturaron para decirnos que pueden hacer lo que quieran con cualquiera de nosotros, el estudiante Julio César fue el medio para un mensaje sangriento, inconcebible.

Mi tierra es un campo de hojas secas que cubren infinidad de huesos, sangre que escurre hacia los ríos en los que jugábamos cuando éramos niños, hojas secas que cubren expedientes sin resolver, los cuerpos de miles de mujeres asesinadas porque en muchos de los estados el concepto de feminicidio ni siquiera se considera en los códigos legales, para ellos las mujeres mueren por violencia entre la pareja, prostitución, accidentes o suicidio. Irónico y triste.

Bajo la hojarasca hay rostros que están dormidos fatalmente, pozos en los que han sido disueltos sus brazos, las piernas que todavía hubieran recorrido tantos caminos, en esa tierra húmeda y helada esperan los que han sido arrancados de sus familias, tienen la mandíbula trabada por el dolor que han sufrido antes de que les llegara el consuelo de la muerte, tienen los brazos atados, las bocas cubiertas. No pueden hablar a menos que los que estamos en esta orilla les prestemos la voz, le hagamos eco a sus gritos, nadie debería irse de este mundo sin haber sido escuchado y reconfortado, sin que se le haya hecho justicia.

Observo la sonrisa de Julio César en una fotografía de Internet, imagino a todos los estudiantes a los que no podrá dar clases, la escuela por la que no podrá caminar ni las tardes en que le contaría a su hija historias para que deje de llorar, no podrá alzarla entre la copa de los árboles y decirle que es un pájaro, no podrán descubrir el sol ni las nubes entre las ramas, no volverá a ver a su hija porque le arrancaron las alas y el rostro, Julio cayó bajo las hojas secas, ahora espera el cerillo, el incendio que se lleve de una maldita vez a los que nos han desfigurado la alegría, las llamas del cambio que ya hierve en nosotros...

Javier Tinajero Rodriguez

<u>Tu voz</u>
(Hacia una resistencia creativa)

"Nosotros, los sobrevivientes,
¿A quiénes debemos la sobrevida?
¿Quién se murió por mí en la ergástula,
quién recibió la bala mía,
la para mí, en su corazón?"
Roberto Fernández Retamar

Hoy no vengo aquí como un poeta
me quito todas las pretensiones
me aparto de todas las etiquetas
me desprendo de estas gafas empañadas de prejuicios
me saco este rostro avergonzado y atribulado
me arranco el cabello, la piel y la mísera carne
para mostrar mis huesos
y hallar las nubes.

Sí, más allá del tuétano
y de la oscuridad en la tumba
hay hermosas nubes.

Hoy vine aquí como un hombre común
me esfuerzo por quitarme esta ropa llena de rabia
me marcho del deseo de violencia
me extirpo los dientes de la venganza
me despojo de la imbecilidad
renuncio al miedo
y me libero del nombre y de todo lo que estorbe
sólo para dejar esta voz
tu voz
que por diminuta que sea
ha decidido llegar aquí a romper el silencio
el silencio complaciente
el silencio de la incertidumbre
el silencio atroz de la diaria agonía
y el silencio de la insaciable muerte.

Esta voz
tu voz
que por invisible que sea
se escuche a sí misma:
pensar
      crear
          resistir
y enciendo y entiendo estas palabras como velas
como lámparas que puedan alumbrar en la oscuridad de los días
una por cada nombre
cada hijo
cada hermana
cada padre
cada madre y cada uno de todos los que faltan:

¿Dónde puedo encontrarte?
¿En qué forma, a qué distancia me necesitas?
Escribo en voz alta:
Pensar para crear es resistir.
Porque hay que buscar
                encontrar
ante los desparecidos
ante la sangre que escupe la tierra
ante la ignorancia obtusa
ante la bestia que come sin hambre
ante la tristeza inmóvil
ante las esperanzas aplastadas
ante las ideas enterradas
ante los asesinos
ante los muertos
ante el dolor del dolor
hay que enseñar
una forma certera de caminar:
pensar
      crear
          resistir
y embisto estas palabras como un manifiesto del quehacer poético
para demostrar que la desdicha puede aliviarse
y que no hay otro camino que hablar claro:
No vayas con los ojos cerrados
ve con los pies

con las manos abiertas
unámonos y dejemos de ser rehenes de esta realidad sinsentido
y hagamos una resistencia pensante y creativa
para que la libertad deje de ser sólo un sustantivo abstracto
para descubrir algo que derribe a la indiferencia
para inspirar al monstruo aciago de la idiotez
para hallar el sitio en dónde aniquilar la apatía
para dejar de comer el desaliento
pensar
  crear
    resistir
ante el absurdo de la vida
pensar
  crear
    resistir
y encontrar el asombro
pensar
  crear
    resistir
con la poesía que respira
pensar
  crear
    resistir
con la lucidez que nace poema
pensar
  crear
    resistir
y decir la verdad.

Chuck Taylor

Making Flags Real

All nations should make their flags from the skins of their slaughtered soldiers just off the battlefields. These soldiers would have in their pockets signed consent forms saying that their dried and cured skins be sewn and dyed for patriotic purpose. No one values peace more than a soldier, and to see the dead skins of our nation's soldiers waving high at major events, football games and graduations, would be a perfect reminder that patriotism has no connection to war. The patriot's heart glows when he moves into the Rocky Mountains. The patriot's spirit soars when he watches the movie Citizen Kane, listens to Aaron Copeland's Appalachian Spring, or reads Sandra Cisneros' House on Mango Street, for the patriot then can sees his land is capable of greatness and was not made for destruction. The patriot cries when war arrives, whether the war can find justification or not.

Chuck Taylor

NRA Ode

I dream natural selection where all those under one hundred years of age in the NRA are drafted into the army and put in the front lines of battle. We are running short on volunteers, and 2nd and 3rd tour National Guarders, haven't most of them killed themselves?

This will be a dream come true, a fine test of manhood or womanhood, and a wonderful hunting experience with plenty of prey that deserve to be killed where you won't have to dress the meat for eating after the kill, and that's such a pain, as you know.

Trophies, of course, remain an old military tradition going back to the beginning of armies, but if you are an NRA'er you've probably got deer antlers up your ass. I can see erect enemy dicks straight from the taxidermist onto American walls.

Yes, here's a dream come true for lovers of guns, that cold hard steel, can it be pulled from their hands? And here's paradoxically a little socialism supporting free enterprise: free VA hospital treatments for the rest of their lives.

Juan Carlos Castrillón

Por Xánath Caraza

Espuma sangrante
Para los 43 estudiantes de Ayotzinapa

Este mar que lame el arena
Olas hambrientas
Testigos sonoros
Luna de agua con ojos quietos
Inmóviles palmeras mudas frente a mí
Caminan los rayos del amanecer en las calles
Marchan ante el contenido rugido del mar
Aves migratorias en el horizonte
Con ellas vuelo
Arena salmón lamida por la espuma sangrante
Mientras cuarenta y tres niños perdidos
Gritan en tus líquidas rojas entrañas
Aullidos sordos, aullidos sordos
En este mar estático que ruge
Ruge mar, ruge, ruge sus nombres
Para la eternidad

ESPOSONTLI
Traducido al náhuatl por Tirso Bautista Cárdenas

Ompuali uan eyi Ayotzinapa momachtianij

Ni ueyiatl tlen ki pipitsoa xalli
mayantomonatl
tsilintlachianij
Mestliatl ika moseiujtokej ixtiolli
Ueyapacmej mokamatsakuaj no ixpa
Ipan kayejtipa mo nejnemiltiaj yaultsinko tlauil
Nejenmij imelaj kuakuatakankayotl ueyiatl
Nejnenmijtotomej ipan ueyiljuikatl
Ininuaya ni patlani
Chilkostikxalli tlen ki pipitsoa esposontli
Kema ompualuaneyi konemej polojtokej
Kuatsajtsij ipan mo chichiltikijtiko
Ijtikotsajtsilis, ijtikotsajtisilis
Ipan ni moseuijtokatl tlen kuakuataka
Xikuakuataka ueyiatl,xi kuakuataka, xi kuakuataka, xi kukuataka
inin tokayotl
Ipan nochi yolistli.

44

Mariah Stettner

Moments of Imperfection

Drops of paint fall
from the tip of my brush
because my hand stalls
in midair, waiting
for some imaginary bell
to sound that tells me
She is perfect, but
canvas breathes moments
of imperfection that mirror
Skin because canvas sees
only brushstroke and color
and too many eyes see
Color, only Color.

So my brush
drips red, and I wonder
if this is the color that blood
makes as it pools on sidewalks
riddled with people who see
Monochromatically.

Nazario Soto Minero

<u>Son de ayotzinapa</u>

Aunque lo maten
Aunque lo asesinen
Aunque lo exterminen
como desde hace siglos
Aunque lo masacren
El pueblo vencerá.

La clase opresora
debe comprender
que el afán genocida
ha llegado a su límite
El estado represivo no puede durar
sus lujos suicidas
no son eternos
La enfermiza decadencia de su sociedad
finalmente
será superada por el amor de los que luchan.

El brazo ejecutor
Las fuerzas represoras
Los asesinos a sueldo
Los sucios verdugos
Los que aprietan cobardemente el gatillo
obedeciendo
"órdenes superiores"
No podrán vivir
No podrán soñar
No podrán dormir
Ni cantar
Ni escupir
No podrán llorar
Ni odiar
sin sentir sobre sus cráneos grotezcos
la gota ecocida de la culpabilidad.

Aquél que asesina a su propia raza estará por siempre maldito.

Sus amos
Los que lamen sangre
por un mísero sueldo
Los que estudian y conspiran
para organizar la explotación
y hacer redituable la ignominia
Los robots de carne y hueso
Los vampiros de su entraña
Los depredadores de sí mismos
están condenados a desaparecer
Sólo serán parte
de un remoto pasado
ridículamente caníbal.

Y los propagandistas
Los mentirosos
Los que ponen la sonrisa
para engañar despóticamente
Los que justifican la matanza
limpian las huellas
defienden la podredumbre
tergiversan los hechos
Esos y esas
que utilizan la fina corbata
o el collar de perlas
como cadena umbilical
para sus dueños
No podrán comer
No podrán beber
ni imaginar
ni escribir
ni leer
No podrán besar
ni acariciar
ni escuchar
No podrán hablar
ni siquiera podrán defecar
sin que el retortijón mortífero
del remordimiento
les recuerde su enorme bajeza.

Nosotros
Los trabajadores
Los que nos levantamos antes del alba
para sudar alegres nuestro pan
Los únicos creadores
de toda la riqueza material y espiritual
sobre la faz de la tierra
Los que amamos la vida viviendo
Los que acompañamos nuestras penas
mutuamente
y nos reconocemos
como miembros destacados
de una misma especie
Los y las del corazón henchido
contra las adversidades
Nosotros
Nosotras
que nos apoyamos solidarios
en nuestra necesidad
Pronto
ahora mismo
sabremos organizarnos
equitativamente
para anular
por siempre
el largo periodo
de la sangrienta obscuridad.

La historia es nuestra
El rechazo a ser esclavo
es lo que realmente
cambia al mundo.

Erika Said

Ser de ningún lado

en donde estoy parada no alcanza a observarse
el ondular de ninguna bandera
no hay país que se haga cargo de mí
vivo en el campoabierto del miedo
sin nombre y sin amigos
vivo bajo el cielo de la duda

no soy de ningún lado
no sé a dónde me dirijo o si llegaré
a la tierra que me han prometido el cine
y la televisión
las casas de cinco habitaciones
con jardín y cochera
en los catálogos en las revistas habitadas
por modelos de ojos azulados
cabello castaño
piel que una vez fue blanca
tostada artificialmente
ahora oscura como la piel mía
de genes tropicales
diseñada para andar a merced del sol

hoy no encuentro mi camino
estoy en el desierto de la incertidumbre
no sé para dónde voy
no sé si cuando llegue
sabré que he llegado

y eso que no vengo de lejos
apenas unos kilómetros río abajo
y eso que también soy ser de vuelos
pero intuyo
que el volar
se prolongará toda una vida
mis alas andarán cansadas por las nubes
pero sin aduanas ni reglamentos
y aunque libre
me acompañará siempre alguna búsqueda
alguna angustia
de pertenecer
siempre a ningún lado.

M. Miranda Maloney

<u>Plucked</u>

After the femicides, Cd Juárez, MX
In the middle of our lives
the sky comes down wide at the mouth
You are not among the winter trees
You are not among the narrow streets
And the routine path of your walk
with your hair draped around your shoulders
barely a woman trusting the desire in songs
trusting the streets of our city—
paper boys, street vendors,
rush of traffic
Those who see you last
point to this corner—frame of
gas stations, birds bathing in the winter light,
yellow wrappers, whir of footsteps
A slur of a slow moving car pushes
against the curbside where you stand
unwrapping candy, and in a blink
of a lash, you are gone
And when the sky breaks open
in a blue-black night, I stand at the door,
as I will forever stand, waiting
dreaming you are alive, somewhere crying

[message]

1

Eyes closed limbs stiff on a bed you died
a sweet death at the wake of sky thick
black smoke severed breasts & semi-automatics
discharge by broken children & santa muerte cocaina
strung devotees in sects who butcher & sacrifice
for the faithful promise cocaine of clichés: big house
big truck big stamp of drug lords carved on bones
to scare the hell out of old ladies with their message:
keep your prayers flags anthems rallies this won't do
the children & women & you on the way to dust

2

Abuela, my love, it's a good thing you died
& everything is just like the last: dark remains unpunished
while the sun doesn't touch deeper than the skyline.
I pray the way you taught me:
Ave Maria, send down a spiral of whoop ass
upon those who defecate your country.
Amen.

3

tears of mothers swell of flesh
piss of dogs flags of pride
bullets of lords ache of grandmothers
& armies starved mother country
who guards your streets of cocaine
& decay?

Part II

"Revolution is not a one time event."--Audrey lorde

Pilar Rodríguez Aranda

<u>De ejecuciones y engaños</u>

A muy corta distancia
el ejército corrupto y cruel de nuestro México
La corbata manchada de todo político y la pantalla en todo teléfono
a muy corta distancia
La guerra continúa y ya nadie dice nada
Decenas de muertos al día
criminales, dicen
¿Y los otros? las mujeres los migrantes
los indígenas los periodistas los activistas los niños
los independientes los pensantes
En un sistema de clones y de cáncer
alarmante ceguera la de todos
Es mutismo o acaso crónica sordera
Que me expliquen Tlatlaya y Villas de Salvárcar cinco años de
diferencia
y nadie lleva la cuenta
Ya no cuenta
Normalización de la telenovela Noticias de malos contra buenos
Dios contra mí y contra ti también

No lo dudes
Sus sotanas son para cubrir su falsedad
Templos de hipocresía y control
Castigo de oratoria y perdón garantizado aunque no cumplas tu
penitencia
porque todos son pecadores y acabarán en el infierno que proponen
Su imaginación habrá de crear esa calurosa dimensión
para su sobre/post/vivencia
A muy corta distancia
se encuentra el karma

consecuencia onda de la que no se escapa
Lo que generamos cuenta
Nos regresa de acuerdo a la fuerza conque fue realizada
Piedra lanzada Bloque de cemento hundido
Este país, una farsa que aceptamos gobierno que no representa
ni es electo

Cada voto no cuenta A muy corta distancia nada cuenta
ni los muertos
ni los milagros
ni los desaparecidos
Lo único que sí cuenta
es la corta distancia
hasta el silencio y el olvido.

Of Executions and Deceptions

At a very short distance our Mexico's army Corrupt and cruel
The stained tie of every politician and the screen on every phone at a
very short distance
War goes on and no one says a thing Tens of deaths every day
criminals, they say
And the others? the women the migrants the natives
the newspeople the activists
the children

the independent the thinkers
In a system of clones and cancer alarming blindness of them all
Mutism or maybe chronic deafness
Explain to me Tlatlaya and Villas de Salvárcar five years of difference
and no one is keeping count
It doesn't count any more
Normalisation of the soap opera
News of the bad ones against the good ones
God against me and against you too
Do not doubt
With soutanes they cover their falseness
Temples of hypocrisy and control
Oratory's punishment and guaranteed pardon even if you don't keep
your penance
because they are all sinners and will end in the hell
they propose
Their imagination will create this warm dimension
for their sur/post/vival
At a very short distance
one finds karma
consequence wave one can't escape from

What we generate counts
It comes back according to the force with which it was executed
Stone thrown Cement block sunken
This country, a farce we accept government which doesn't represent
nor is elected
Every vote does not count At a very short distance nothing counts
not even the deaths nor the miracles
nor the disappeared
The only thing that counts is how short is the distance of silence and
oblivion.

La bestia

Se entromete entre comidas como tema de conversación
Barullo de cientos: cada vez menos
lugar para vivir en paz
La huida es el llamado y la pantalla nos hace ojitos
para que sigamos la vía de la mentira que brilla
como los espejos que los conquistadores nos daban
La diferencia es que ahora pagamos por ellos
más que la vida
La bestia ruge llamando
Vidas y piernas entre sueños y pesadillas hay
gente amable y gente ruin
Niños que abandonarán sus cuerpos
y ni siquiera sabrán de su adultez
O quizá ya supieron demasiado
Vagones de inocencia manchada por nuestra ceguera
Quebrado envase de odio y quimera
Pretenden alcanzar al padre o buscar una vida nueva
Otra, la que sea
Apilados en el piso y limpios de lágrimas sin fin
Algunos son devueltos a la bestialidad
de una cotidianidad donde trabajar todo el día
no alcanza para sobrevivir
y la muerte los espera a la vuelta de toda esquina
Por eso se atreven e intentan llegar hasta el norte
aunque eso pueda significar
ser violado por el pollero
o terminar en una bolsa enterrado
sin nombre
La bestia detrás de cada curva penetrando cada poro
Absorbiendo cualquier resquicio de niñez
La bestia también se apropia de mi nombre
Nubla mis ojos y me paraliza
No me queda ni siquiera un tantito ya de fe
Inútil pretender actuar
posteando noticias, fotos y videos

El activismo de hoy también es simulacro
La bestia atrapa niños en su tela de falsa factura
Pretenden llegar a Minnesota desafiando lo desconocido

ver lo que en la tele les dijeron era el éxito
La bestia se los traga con su hipócrita frontera
que pule bien el miedo y se disfraza
La muerte danza entre los dientes tras las cejas
Mirando el mundo humano que es la bestia
sin oídos ni compases compasivos
sólo acordes sin ton/o ni son
La bestia explota y la pateamos para que se calle
y nos deje llegar al trabajo o dormir en la noche
La escondemos debajo de la cama
Nos deporta el descaro de un sistema
asesino que nos niega
Nos negamos y auto-destruimos como los otros
Millones que mueren o se matan
por un solo Slim, un solo Chapo, un solo Peña
En el poder exclaman para contener una bestia amplificada
que rueda y rueda tras las vías
Disfrazada de bondad
La bestia ni llora ni ríe
Es indiferente (como tú y como yo)
Como el alienígena de aquella película
Ese que crece por dentro y luego sale del pecho
como corazón trocado en dragón alado, traicionero
La bestia engaña y arrulla al ángel de la guarda
que al dormirse deja caer ese cuerpo
que queda mutilado
La bestia lo hace picadillo y lo arrastra
No lo protegen ni sus padres ni su dios ni su presidente
Pierde ambas piernas mas no pierde su esperanza
La bestia no los alcanza
los niega
Niños en manos de una despedida constante
De por vida marcado queda el cuerpo
Acaso el alma llega intacta
luego de abordar la amarga hilera
Aunque luego acabe sola y el cuerpo
quede ahogado en un río norteño
o a medio enterrar en el desierto
Allá será mejor, -quieren/necesitan creerlo-
Mantra sin eco: cerebro deslave: túnel estrecho
La consigna de la bestia es la anestesia

Multifacético cuento de hadas
Apatía y terror en uniforme
Las múltiples vistas de la bestia: corte
y solitaria confección de nuestros cuerpos
Bestia que todos contenemos
Los uniformados los bajan "a vergazos" y les roban
Los niños regresan a la Bestia, corren
suben las escaleras, ella los acepta
Sobre la bestia planean por segundos se despegan
de esta realidad oscura y mortal que dura eterna
Ya no hay regreso y la bestia los adopta
los adapta y los destruye
La bestia no sabe de alabanzas
no reza ni escucha ni se detiene
Tampoco alberga los recuerdos
Es de fierro, y pesa
Te entrega, te traga, te desaparece, te encierra
En su enorme panza de hambre y chemo
Se lleva al perro niño
Ese niño que es ahora también, un poco bestia.

The beast

It meddles in between meals as topic of conversation
Racket of hundreds: every time there are less
places to live in peace
The fleeing is the calling and the screen beckons us
and we continue the path of the shining lie
like the mirrors the conquerors would give us
The difference is now we pay for them
more than life
The beast roars calling
Lives and legs in between dreams and nightmares there are
kind people and mean people
Children who will abandon their bodies
and will never even know their adulthood
Or maybe they already know too much
Freight cars of innocence stained by our blindness
Broken container of hate and chimera
They mean to catch up with the father or find a new life
Another one, any life
Piled on the floor and cleaned by endless tears
Some are sent back to the bestiality
of an everyday life where working all day long
is not enough to survive
and death awaits for them at the turn or every corner
That is why they dare try getting to the North
even though this might result
on being raped by the pollero
or end buried inside a bag
with no name
The beast behind
every curve
penetrating every pore
Absorbing all trace of childhood
The beast also runs off with my name
Clouds my eyes and paralyses me
I haven't got left much faith
It is useless pretending to act
To post news, photos and videos
The activism of today is also a sham
The beast traps the children in its false making web

They intend to reach Minnesota defying the unknown
and see what in tv they were told was success
The beast swallows them with its hypocritical border
which polishes fear so well and dresses itself up
Death dances in between teeth behind the eyebrows
Looking at the human world which is the beast
with no ears or compassionate compasses
only chords with sense-less tones
The beast explodes and we kick it so it will shut down
and let us get to work or sleep at night
We hide it under the bed
We are deported by the nerve of a system
murderer who denies us
We deny ourselves and self-destroy like the other
Millions who die or kill each other
for a single Slim, a single Chapo, a single Peña
In power they exclaim in order to contain an amplified beast
going round and round after the tracks
Disguised in kindness
The beast doesn't cry nor laughs
It is indifferent (like you and me)
Like that alien from the movie
The one which grows within and comes out of the breast
like a heart turned into a treacherous, winged dragon
The beast fools and lulls the guardian angel
who falls asleep and lets the body fall
left mutilated
The beast chops him and drags her
Not protected by their parents or their god or president
They loose both legs but not their hope
The beast can't reach them
Can only deny them
Children in the hands of a constant farewell
For life the body is left scarred
Maybe the soul arrives intact
after boarding the bitter line
Even if later ends up alone and the body
is left drowned in some Northern river
or half buried in the desert
It will be better there, -they want/need to believe that-
Mantra with no echo: landslide brain: narrow tunnel

The beast's instruction is anaesthesia
Multifaceted fairy tale
Apathy and terror in uniform
The multiple sights of the beast: lonesome
dressmaking of our bodies
Beast we all contain
The uniformed bring them down "a vergazos" to rob them
The children run
They return to the Beast
go up the ladder
It takes them in
Over the beast they soar for seconds they take off
from this dark and mortal reality which lasts eternal
There is no coming back and the beast adopts them
adapts them and destroys them
The beast knows nothing of praises
she doesn't pray nor listens nor stops
Neither does she harbour any memories
She's made of iron, and is heavy
She delivers you, swallows you, disappears you, locks you up
In its huge belly of hunger and chemo*
It takes with it the dog child
That child who is also, now, a bit beastly.

Farwa Naqvi

I Refuse.

I refuse to apologize for looking like someone who
did something awful. Every time some foolish group of men,
emboldened by the power handed to them by their imaginary god
or political faction, takes up a sword or a gun or a machete, you look
upon me with suspicion. You look at me with anger. You look at me
with hate. And unless I bow down, in the same stance of supplication
taken by those violent animals that call themselves Muslim, and
declare once again that, "I am not of them," I will be considered
guilty. And why?
Because I am brown and this is my cross to bear the way
being an "illegal" is that of another shade, being a "thug" is that of
yet one more? I am tired of being eyeballed for looking like you
think a Muslim looks when most of you, lets admit it now, couldn't
find the country I'm from on a map made for children. Yet you pass
along your ignorance and bile to your own children who point at
me and sneer, "Osama." What do they know of the world before 9/11
made anyone remotely associated with the vast region of the entire
Indian Subcontinent and Middle East fair game for unfair hate?
They know the video of foolish men in funny hats doing bad things,
squeezed in between the high speed car chase and the celebrity
"news." They know the scandalous, the titillating, but never the fair,
hardly the balanced. But what of them, they are innocents. What do
you know of the Sikh gurdwaras you deface, what do you know of the
difference between Libya and Jordan and Bangladesh and Sudan?
No, they are not all the same and how can you still not
know that? How, in the age of information and previously
unimaginable global intimacy can you still not know that they are
not synonymous? With only a few taps of your keyboard, you can see
beheadings and spread hate, yet, you cannot see that there is a vast
world you are pigeonholing with your ignorance?
It's been nearly fourteen years since a group of foolish men
brought the fury of the West upon an entire religion and anyone
who looks kinda-sorta like your vision of them, yet how is it you still
need to be reminded that we're not all the same? Since the latest,
nauseating, abhorrent hijacking of decency by the foolish

men of ISIS, there is a rash of op-eds and interviews where Muslim PR people decry the actions of the heathens, remind the world how many millions of Muslims are on the globe, how unique they all are, how distant from those gun wielding foolish men. And after what seems like the billionth time an obviously non-radical, non-insane person tries to explain the insanity of clumping together of a population of same-faith folks, you still don't get it. So they must whip out simplistic comparisons to convey the absurdity, "well, Hitler called himself Christian...does that make all Christians evil?" "Please remember, the Crusades were in the name of a religion." "Well, righteous Christian white people used to burn black folks alive just a few decades ago, should I be afraid of them all?" "Are Catholics from Mexico, America, Italy, and South Africa identical?" Why must we still do this? How do you still not understand? I refuse to dignify your ignorance.

Now let's move on to the Sikhs, and Hindus, the Baha'is and Catholics and Christians. And even those that secretly hold no faith. They kinda-sorta look like Muslims too, so they now have to send out the PR people to say, "hey, hey now, we look similar but we REALLY aren't like them. To which the worst of you will respond to the likes of, "I don't care. They're all the same, those camel fucking towel heads." No. We're not. I refuse to be inconvenienced any longer. If you haven't figured out the difference between geography and religion, culture and faith, crazy and non-crazy then I refuse to try to explain it.

Do you not see the irony of your hate? Those foolish factions group together all they have unfairly condemned, too blinded to see individual children of the god they claim to love. And so it is with you. Some of them spill the blood of innocents in repayment for some conceived wrong. And so it is with a few of you. Feeling holier-than-thou and compelled by revenge, you hurt, destroy, kill that which resembles, but is certainly not, the culprit. I refuse to look past your hypocrisy.

And I refuse to tolerate the subtle intolerance either - so carefully wrapped in the cloak of political correctness. The "so, where are you from?" before I've even finished introducing myself followed by the "no, where are you from?" I'm from my mother's uterus, let's now move on. For when I ask you such a question and

63

you name a place, I take your word for it. I do not interrogate you. I refuse to let you make me nervously question whether I should say "Texas" or "Louisiana" - both accurate - when obviously you want to know why I'm brown. I refuse to let you bully me to say Pakistan so that you can put me in that pigeonhole, so you can invalidate everything else that I am in order to have a "polite" discussion about my family's migratory history, my accent or lack thereof, my feelings about ISIS all while "welcoming" me to my own country. I refuse to let you dictate the conversation. Talk to me long enough, as you would any other person, and my complex history, my heritage, my pride at being Pakistani American will come up. But you just can't wait to make the connection, to simplify my identity, oh so politely. What do you get out of it, exactly, when I finally identify the origins of my brownness? It's not like you could tell me which current horror story originates from that country or how it relates to Osama or ISIS. I refuse to play your subtle race games unless you can find Pakistan on a globe for me. If you can't, you owe me money for my time and irritation.

And you. You other shades of brown. How dare you? You know what it is like to be done wrong. And still, with one breath you protest the indignity and injustice of being called a wetback and with the next you find it hilarious to call anything you think may possibly, perhaps, perchance be from over "there" a "terrorist"? You take to the streets, my darker brothers and sisters, chanting that #blacklivesmatter, and they do - I chant with you - yet, you think it ok to ridicule me despite not knowing who I am or where I am "from?" And YOU. You Muslims and Hindus, you Pakistanis and Arabs, after going through all of this - YOU still have the audacity to racially profile anyone?

Nah, the thing is you're not thinking. Not enough of us are thinking, and that is the problem. Because, you see, once you start thinking - beyond the indoctrinated, tribal brainwashing - you can't stop. Once you start questioning what you've been told, what you've been led to believe, you start realizing the answers are far more complex. And it's a lot harder to deal with the complexities of the real human condition than to think, 'towelhead.' And who wants to make life harder than it is? Well, you and your ignorance are making my life harder and I refuse to let you any longer. I refuse.

Jasminne Mendez

No Más Racismo RD

Are you, are you
Coming to the tree
They strung up a man
They say who murdered three.
Strange things did happen here
No stranger would it be
If we met at midnight.
In the hanging tree.
Are you, are you
Coming to the tree
Where the dead man called out
For his love to flee.
Strange
strange
strange
strange fruit hangin from popular trees
Dominican trees bear a strange fruit
Blood on the leaves and blood at the root
Black Haitian bodies swingin' in the Island breeze
a piece of strange fruit hanging from a mango tree
strange fruit in the center of
santiago's square
and the police didn't care
that he wasn't supposed to be there
Just one
One too many
Tulile
A shoe shiner
who probably said sí señor
and no señora
and smiled vaguely when you didn't tip
him
and felt the stares now that
he wasn't a citizen
and the U.S. Mexico border
isn't the only one out of order
43 displaced, misplaced cuerpos

in Mexico
#yamecanse
like 200,000 displaced, erased ciudadanos
of Dominican Haitian descent
nomasracismoRD
Descending on the barrios
of their birth
their birthright
stripped from them like
stolen goods on a thief
but it was nothing they took
it was nothing he stole
Tulile
hanging from a tree
For a robbery
they claim
but can't maintain
the lies they've
told themselves
for centuries.
we are of indian ancestry
african blood don't run in
our veins
but can't hide the skin
that you live in
but we label ourselves Tainos
and spaniards
nothing like those Haitian
bastards
who come to
steal the jobs
we don't want
to work in the sun
that will make our complexion darker
a marker and target
for hate
But lynching him won't change
the history of your name
and this isn't a game of white vs black
this is modern day black on black crime
of the worst kind

anyone born of illegal immigrants
after 1929
listen to me carefully
let me make myself clear
you are not wanted here
you newly undocumented
who taint our cities
with your smells and santeria
and speak a language
we don't understand
and can't wait to ban you
from our
streets
and our schools
and the place
you call
home
But I, a full blooded Dominicana
know it isn't right
and I will use my wisdom and my words to fight
the brutality
of the men in power who
stand by and do nothing
while evil prevails
and the government fails
to indict and give
sight to the plight
of natural born citizens
whose only sin
is their darker skin
and I want to hang a noose
around your ignorance
and flippant
apathy towards
basic human dignity
because your affinity for
racism wears the noble mask of
good-intentions while you prey like leeches
on the very people and natives you fail
to mention in your
election speeches

and you take their lack of education
and chronic starvation
and lead them to believe that
their neighbor
is the enemy
ignoring the fact that this dystopian reality
is caused by your inability to
find an end to the 3rd world poverty
to feed the hungry
or clothe the poor
so instead you have them point a finger
and push the enemy out the door
but before the bitter fruit can be eaten alive
they will find a place to run, so that they
can finally be free...
because they don't want to be
to be the next bitter crop
hanging from a tree, for the sun to rot
for the tree to drop
like a piece of strange fruit
barely dangling in the island breeze
of an untouched mango tree.

When Was the Last Time You Saw A Black Boy Smile?
(In response to Pedro Pietri's poem: When Was the Last Time You Saw Mami Smile?)

He ran from the crib to the cradle
Breathless
As his daddy smiled
So he smiled too

He read a book about a fish
One
Two
Three
A, B, C
Gasping for air
And the teacher smiled
So he smiled too

There was a momma
And a Nana
And a brother
And a sister
And cousins
And boyfriends
And Sister's baby
And...

And a small house
With too few rooms
Bars and locks on the door
And no daddy anymore

But this little black boy
Found the strength
To inhale
Exhale
And smile

When he didn't pass the test
And was expelled for attention deficit
His mama threw a fit

But there was nothing he'd regret
So he sighed with relief
And smiled

No money coming in
Every day he'd go out
Get ignored by most
Accosted by some
But never treated fairly
And he barely
Had any patience left
For smiling

He tried to get a job
Was told he looked like a slob
Cause his pants hung low
And he spoke too slow
So he left without a word
Huffing and puffing
Until he finally
Stopped smiling

Because his sister needed to get fed
And his mom was sick in bed
And the lights were out
And he wanted to shout
But couldn't find the words
Because they stuck to his chest
And collapsed in his lungs

And he wanted them to understand

But he was
Questioned by the cops
Cause he lingered too long
In one place
His face
Was a target
For hate
That choked his
Already airless airways

All because
He wouldn't smile

Stopped in the street
Trying to defeat
His predestined fate
Couldn't get it straight
When they asked him his name
So they took out a cane

And…

And look America…
I see him smiling now
And we should never make
Him feel bad again

We'll always give you a chance
And a home
And food
And enough
Enough
Just
Enough

Because…

I can see you from my laptop
I can see you from my phone
I can see you on the news

Smiling
Smiling when they cuffed you
Smiling when they beat you
Smiling
Smiling
Smiling
even
when
you
couldn't breathe

Takeshi Edmundo López

<u>Noticias</u>

"Con Obama o sin Obama
el imperio es el imperio"
Saúl Ibargoyen

6 bramidos lapidaron
el cuerpo fláccido de Brown,
rendido, desarmado,
una saeta metálica
perforó los sueños entre sus ojos.

Hay un títere de ébano
que habla sobre la sombra de la balanza
se ve adornando la silla blanca
de un cuarto ovalado,
se ha olvidado de Malcom,
de King, de Emmett.
Las panteras de su sangre
han cambiado de color.

Pero yo les vengo a hablar
del segundo Brown
-recuerden, no del victorioso-
del que se desplomó en la calle
cuando Wilson de uniforme azul,
de insignia y piel blanca,
decidió que había un delito en la carne,
en su tono oscuro de pobreza
y cayó en un espiral de muerte
el joven Michael.

¿Cuántos frutos extraños más habrá
en las calles, junto a los pájaros,
al mirar las nubes?

Un mazo rompe el silencio,
el sistema acepta su odio:
Wilson, el de uniforme azul,
piel blanca y manos llenas de carmín
sale a cazar con su arma cargada
de barras y estrellas.

La gente siembra la rabia

en la tierra removida por el dolor,
sale a llenar de ecos los bulevares
pero vienen los bárbaros,
con sirenas enloquecidas
de toque de queda,
con toletes vorágines,
con las botas lustradas por el desprecio.
Quieren apagar el llanto,
quieren borrar la sombra,
quieren hundir sus falanges plateadas
y sacarles la memoria.

Esta es la historia:
6 bramidos destrozaron al joven
negro, pobre, desarmado,
libre, hermano Brown.
No hay final.

relámpagos en los ojos

"los que no ignoran de qué cosa está hecho el amor;
que no llevan las manos bocarriba
aunque traigan el alma bocabajo,
son mis hermanos."
Miguel Guardia

Sólo eran jóvenes pobres
hijos de la tierra más flaca
sólo querían dejar de sentir vacío
porque los puentes se habían derrumbado
nadie recordaba que de aquel lado
estaban atrapados ellos
en la más inhumana miseria
como si no fueran nosotros
y no tuvieran ni garganta
ni llanto ni sueños ni sombra ni miedo
eso que nos hace levantar de madrugada
por sentir el cuerpo suicidándose
hacia arriba

Traían libros no fusiles
traían las manos llagadas por el arado
toscas duras por tanta pobreza
aún así los detuvieron
hombres con el mismo color de maíz
con sus mismos nombres
con el mismo fuego del hambre
devorando sus estómagos
pero sin brillo en los ojos
lo cambiaron por un papel con números
un casco y un tolete
Se olvidaron de Lucio y de Genaro
les escupieron plomo
y se los llevaron
y quieren que olvidemos sus rostros
y nos faltan
y los buscamos
porque sentimos rabia

Sólo querían decirles a los más chicos
que merecen el mundo
que entre más libros menos miseria
que no son carne para el dolor
que en ellos está la semilla del Héroe verdadero

Quieren que nos olvidemos de 43 caras
¿qué padre olvida el rostro de su hijo?
¿cómo llorarle al vapor al polvo
al hueco en el piso a las cajas vacías?
¿por qué no nos quieren decir
adónde los llevó su doctrina del odio?

Eran como también lo fuimos
como lo somos
jóvenes con relámpagos en los ojos
con el corazón blanco
con la esperanza intacta
con las lámparas encendidas

¿Por qué me levanto últimamente
con ganas de salir y gritar por las calles
sus nombres sus millones de nombres?
¿por qué me despierto en estos días
sintiéndome desaparecido?

Manuel Martinez

From Los Duros (Floricanto, 2014)
Police Interrogation Scene

How You Get an Indio to Talk

School goes on. There's yellow tape that says DO NOT CROSS POLICE LINE around the burned building. Everything smells like ashes. It's a scar now, black and gray, the roof falling down. The school isn't beautiful anymore. It's ugly like Los Duros, like the ugly, broken houses of Thermal and Mecca. It wasn't right anyway, that the school was perfect and untouched. All it did was remind us that what lay outside was sick and ugly.

Today, I walk the halls listening. There's worried talks between the others, questions about where families will go, about the protest and whether it should still go on, about Teacher, about the fire. No one seems to know anything. They don't tell us anything here. In one class, a girl asks a teacher for the truth. But she doesn't answer anything. She says, "don't worry about those things. Let Principal Joe and your parents worry about these things. The police will find who did it."

No one here says anything worth hearing. I won't come back. When the others have begun to gather around at lunch, I head for the gate that surrounds the school that they lock during the day so that no one can leave. There's a school policeman on a bike watching. He wears dark sunglasses so that we can't see who he's got his eyes on. He's watching with suspicion, believing that someone here's set the fire and is planning something else. He doesn't know who, but he has his ideas. He looks like he wants to kill everyone.

I head for the small opening in the fence, and from behind I hear the policeman say, "Hey, where do you think you're going?" When I don't stop, he yells again, "Hold it right there! I'm talking to you, damn it!" But I don't stop. I can't stay here even a minute longer and his voice is full of fury because I won't obey. I hurry now, because I'm suddenly sure that he will kill me, that he's going to take his stick and beat me until I disappear into the sand. I struggle at the opening. It's not big enough to walk through unless you make yourself small and turn sideways. Before I am through, he's caught up to me on his bike. He jumps from the seat letting the bike fall to the sidewalk in a clatter, and he grabs my shoulders with his heavy hands. He pulls me backwards through the opening, and my head bangs against the metal post and I fall, my head hitting the sidewalk. He puts his knees on my chest, yelling for others to come help. I don't struggle with him. I know I'm caught and that no one can help me now. I hear more yelling and other policemen have come. They pull me up, putting cuffs around my wrists, shoving me. Principal Joe comes running up, yelling "What's going on here? What's the trouble?"

The policeman who stopped me tells him what I've done as the others lead me to Principal Joe's office. They put me in a seat in the hall outside his door. He comes in with the policeman and they walk inside and close the door. Another policeman stands with his back to the wall watching me. "You like burning shit, kid? Don't like it around here? Maybe you think it'd be better to set this thing on fire, huh?" I don't say anything to him. I watch him instead. He's a white man, young, stronger and bigger than the policeman who pulled me down at the fence. He's smiling at me but there's anger in his mouth and eyes. I know that look.

Principal Joe opens his door and says, "Bring him in." I stand up and walk to the door. The young policeman shoves me into the office. The other policeman is sitting against the wall. "Sit there," Principal Joe says pointing to the chair in front of his desk. He doesn't go around it to sit down. Instead, he sits on the corner of the desk on the same side as me.

"Where were you running to, son? Why didn't you stop when Officer Rodriguez told you to? It won't do you any good to stay quiet. We've got a decision to make. We can call in the city police, or you can tell us what's going on."

"You better talk, boy," the older policeman says.

I don't say anything. I sit there trying to keep quiet inside. I'm afraid, afraid like I get when my mother's angry. I can feel blood on my face from the scrape and there's a big lump on the back of my head. My shirt is torn and my face feels hot like I'm going to cry. But I can't do this in front of these men. I try to think about how my grandfather would act.

"Why were you running?" Principal Joe asks again. "Do you know something about this fire?"

"He did it," the young policeman says. "Sure as shit, he did it.

Look at him. He's a classic firebug. Quiet and weird, textbook case."

"Is there any truth in that, son?" Principal Joe asks. "You don't have to lie anymore. If you did it, you might as well fess up and let us help you. It's going to be a lot worse later on. You got anything you want to tell us?"

I shake my head.

"Told you," the older policeman says. "He isn't going to tell us anything. These kids stick together, but he knows. He knows something."

"Weren't you in Mr. Peña's class?" Principal Joe asks. "I think I remember you in there. Makes sense that you're angry about him losing his job. Is that why you did it?"

I don't say anything.

"It's useless. Call the police," Principal Joe says. "Let them handle it."

"What do we tell them he did?"

"Tell them he was attempting to leave school without authorization. Tell them that he resisted when you attempted to apprehend him. Tell them that you think he might know something about the fire."

***

Teacher wants to know what happened. But I don't remember. It's like a dream, moments that fall in together like a roof collapsing. Juan's father, and another man, the legless man who helped the Teacher a couple of times before the fire, in a white van. I remember that. They told Teacher that they found me wandering on the side of the road close to the Salton Sea. "He was just walking around looking like he'd just been drug through hell," the legless man says to Teacher. "He's close to a heatstroke. I saw it every day in Iraq. He's damned lucky we found him. Another couple of hours in this heat and he'd been coyote food."

"Who did this to you?" Teacher wants to know. But I won't tell him because there's something coming for him, a jaguar in the dark. It's set to tear him apart and I won't help the jaguar. What I can remember, I'll keep to myself because what's done can't be undone.

The policemen came, two of them, both in uniforms. The one with the mustache didn't speak to me. The other one, the one whose lips curled up when he talked to me, took me by the collar, his thumb digging into the back of my neck where the school policeman had grabbed me and pulled me down. It hurt, but that's what he wanted. I kept silent. There was nothing to do but hold my tongue. Principal Joe told them, "He may know something about the fire. He's acting like he knows but doesn't want to say. We questioned him, but he's not going to talk to us. Maybe he'll talk to you."

It was hot, the waves of heat rising as we left the building. "You know something, big boy," the policeman with the sneer said as he pushed me inside the car. "You're going to tell us." He shut the door and walked around to the other side. The mustached policeman was already at the wheel.

"What do you think we ought to do with him?" the sneering man said.

The other one didn't look at him. "There's a lot we can do with him. What do you think?"

"Not going to take his ass to juvie, that's for sure. Not by a long damned shot. Let's take him out to the desert and do some aggressive questioning."

They pulled out on the highway that leads to the dunes. I could feel the heat through the window and my stomach tightened like it always does before the blows. I tried to be quiet, to listen not to them, but to listen to my heartbeat, to keep calm. My grandfather taught me that. But I couldn't hear my heart. The policemen didn't say anything more. They drove into the desert, the dunes getting larger. The mustached policeman made a sudden turn and stopped the car, but left it running.

"Real hot out there, chaca. Real hot. You're going to give us someone, by god. You're going to give us the firebug. You can bet your ass that we're going to find the perp and I'm not about to let some sorry-assed wetback Indian, whatever the fuck you are, stand in the way of getting him."

The mustached policeman said, "That's right, son. You better come clean. Tell us what you know. I don't think it was you, but you got to give us something to go by. We know you're living with your teacher. Did he put you up to it? You can trust us. Just give us what we need and we'll take you home."

"He doesn't want to cooperate," the sneering policeman said. "I can tell just by the way he's hunched over back there. You think you're cool? Cool as a cucumber? It's not too fucking cool out there," he said. I said nothing. I kept my eyes focused on the dunes, on the sand blowing over the top, swirling down little by little, and reforming slowly.

The sneering policeman got out of the car and walked around to the back. He opened the trunk and then came to my side. He opened the door. The handcuffs were still on my wrists. He reached in and grabbed me by the torn collar of my shirt. "Get out here, goddamnit. Sweating balls out here, Kimosabe. Now I'm going to put you in a sweatbox. Probably won't work seeing as how you Indians like that sort of thing. Maybe a while in there will loosen that tongue of yours."

He pushed me to the trunk and said, "Get in." I didn't move and he shoved me hard from behind. "Get in, Kimosabe, or I'm going to put you in and I'm going to do it plenty rough." But it was hard because I couldn't use my arms. I leaned over the edge like I was peering inside. And then he kicked the back of my knees and as I began to fall, he pushed me into the trunk. He closed the lid. I heard him go back to his side of the car and get in. It was dark in the trunk and I couldn't hear anything but muffled voices. I lay on my stomach, my hands behind my back, the heat of the sand coming up through the floor of the car. It burned and I tried to move on my side, but I couldn't turn. I began to breathe heavy, a fear that I was being buried. And then the heat, and something like a dream where my head banged against the roof of a shack, hard, making the sound of a fist banged on a table. And then my tongue so thick, and no water, not even spit, and my tongue hanging out like a dog. And then the itching of my scalp and neck and my arms behind me and then struggle and something like flames. Then blackness.

"You going to tell us, boy?"

"He doesn't hear you, Ray."

"He goddamn hears what he wants to hear. You going to give us some information? Or are you going back in that goddamned trunk."

"He's not going to tell you anything. You left him in there too long."

"Not long enough. You tell me what I want to hear."

Silence. And then kicked from behind, and the sand on my face and neck and then rolling in its fire.

"Pushing him down the dunes isn't going to do the trick. This

80

kid probably doesn't even understand what you're asking. We ought to go back and haul that principal up here for wasting our time."

"He knows. Look at him. He fucking knows."

"He doesn't. He would've spilled it by now."

"He knows. He's not going to tell out of spite. Ain't that right, you little spiteful wetback?"

And then the sound of the car driving off through the sand and my hands free and feeling my wrists and then laughing and crying, one starting where the other finished, and then again and again. My tongue so thick, and no water, not even tears. And then the white van, and Juan's father and the legless man.

"Lucky we found you. It won't kill you, a heatstroke, not if you can get some water in time, but you'll feel like hell for a week."

And Teacher. "What happened? Who did this to you? Who took you out there?"

And my tongue thick in its cave, dry, blistered, but not saying anything except, "I won't help the Jaguar."

"What are you talking about, Jaguar?" Teacher kept asking.

"He doesn't know. He's out of his head," the man with no legs told him.

Ulises Paniagua

<u>Camino al nuevo Palashtu</u>

Hoy es templada la noche en que la estirpe de arena
destapa oscura nitidez como cuchillo de perro
en que alquitrana tras puertas los colmillos de pesadilla

Hoy es larga la noche en que el desierto del Néguev se vuelve ronco
-opuesto al púrpura químico del llanto-
y agita en su humanidad
los confines / las aguas / las reconciliaciones / el desencuentro

Es dulce la noche que cierra silenciosa pero alerta
implosionando dolor hacia el sí mismo
ahondando violencia y odio
más allá de la profusa depresión del Jordán

Pero hoy es ayer   Fue ayer
y es la señal del alba que promete la muerte del clavo y la condena
kufiyya que trasparenta   que se vuelve uva   chufa   perfume de
olivo

Es la primera llamarada en los perfumados incendios del almizcle
Pacífico calor que habrá de absorber lo verde de una línea entre las
piedras

Hoy volverá a dibujarse la sonrisa del Palashtu
cuando relumbre la hermosura entre el océano y la maleza
Hoy es la agonía de esta templada noche:
la plácida y extensa tierra recuperada desde las venas del sol.

Gerard Robledo

El Coyote Habla con su cena, II: Madre

II. ...Madre,

if these children had floated a raft across
a blue ocean, not a murky brown river,
they would be known as refugees on television,

not illegal immigrants. I watched
from the soft comfort of my living room. A screen
flooded with adults, parents, a Mayor, free people

& their flags, stopping a bus stuffed with frail, terrified children,
who escaped being buried face down in their uniforms,
or being burned alive, clutching their backpacks

& notepads – young skin fused to metal –
to be welcomed with freezing beds, closed fists & hissing
words pummeling their hearts;

misspelled brown cardboard signs that read:
"Save our children from diseases," – Tiny red, white, and blue
flags in corners – "Our tax money for U!!!,"
"Hell No, Go Home,"
"U.S. Citizens don't get FREE PASS
Y should illegals;"

and a man spitting on another human
face. It is the only thing to make the city apologize, My heart sank
when I watched the video, Mayor Ramos said.

In losing control for that moment unquestionably
that individual gave the city a black eye...
I do want to take this time
on behalf of the City of Murrieta
to give our most sincere apologies...
to Lupillo Rivera.

Madre, his words whipped across
my back...

...like El Coyote, with money   burning holes

in his pockets.

83

Carolyn Adams

Masters of Western Thought

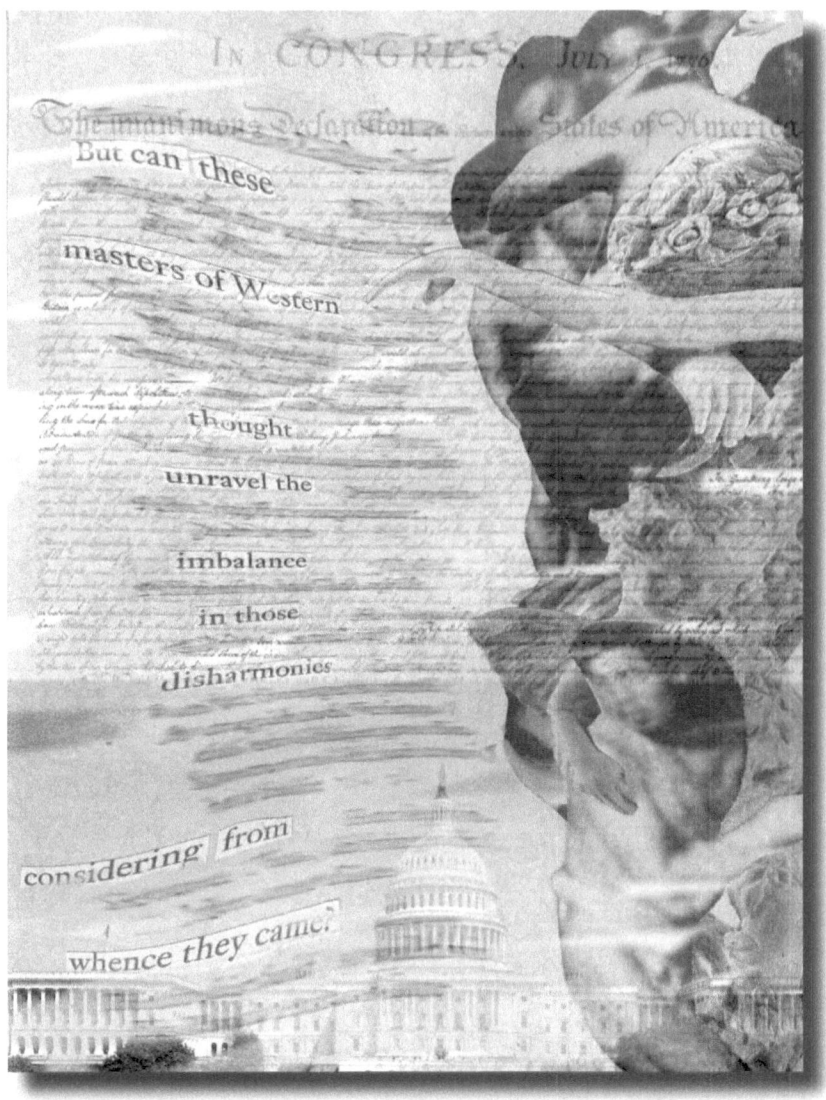

But can these

masters of Western

thought

unravel the

imbalance

in those

disharmonies

considering from

whence they came?

David Sapp

<u>Pardon Me</u>

Please sir, pardon me
for being nothing more
than a meek and skinny girl
from Gaza, Aleppo, Mosul.

A tenant of concrete rubble,
pardon my screams,
my inconsequential dreams,
my tears, my many fears.

Pardon my childish grievance;
I have no opinion, sir;
I'll obey any doctrine and follow
your flag whatever the color.

I've grown accustomed to your bombs,
fiery kisses on the desert sky,
but please sir, and I sincerely
apologize, be so kind and return:

my school, a place
to read and write and play,
to pretend for a fleeting moment,
that I may be a carefree child;

my roof, my walls, a place to eat
to put my few, little trinkets,
a simple room where I might
sleep and whisper close to my sisters;

my brother, his dark,
splendid head, his quick, black eyes;
you see, my mother weeps
for his brilliant, flashing smile;

my arm; there remain
a few things I'd like to hold

a boy I think I'd like to embrace,
and it is arduous with only one;

my innocence; please sir, restore
life to my eyes and modesty
behind my veil, beneath my skirt;
pour purity back into my skin.
Please sir, pardon me.

Bullets

Behind a beige, split-level,
on our unexceptional edge of town,
bang, bang, rat-tat-tat.
I cannot account for all the bullets;
I can tally only these whizzing

from erect barrels, ejaculating lead,
slugs spurting from warm muzzles,
scrawny boys and big brothers,
swaggering in camouflage pants.

Today's carnage, a few, tragic cans,
bang, bang, rat-tat-tat,
neighbors rudely jarred from porch rockers,
babies wrenched from naps,

and my wife, rarely swearing,
bang, bang, rat-tat-tat,
flinching at each report.
Who can listen to Mozart?

When is the trigger pulled
in the vast grooves of guileless minds?
Why place the butt in their hands,
slaughter a solution to life's demands?

Oh, if only these children would
stick to girls' curves and cussing,
pick-up trucks, cigars, huntin' dogs,
smuggling their father's whiskey.

Young man, what will you choose?
Soldier, will your bullets neatly cleave
a convenient gap between
prayers to Allah and Jesus,
slice a new pipeline across the desert,

or will you simply stroll into
grades one or two or three, just up the street?

Bang, bang, rat-tat-tat.
Please! I'd rather not see the news
display your handsome face.

Vanessa Torres

Transformación de los objetos transparentes

El estandarte de la libertad, el mágico símbolo de la palabra y la
libertad
no es más hoy que una masa de papel sucio
lleno de tinta,
de palabras que confunden sus colores
de imágenes arrugadas, informes,
perdidas entre un mundo de mentiras,

En virtud de una cruel mímesis
todos aquellos que vorazmente buscan la verdad
van transformándose,
poco a poco su vida se pone a la medida de insaciables
 y terroristas anuncios de último minuto,
las calles de sus hijos, llenas del miedo del New York times,
de la avaricia televisada, de la sordera que paraliza,
y esa tristeza que nos dice al oído:
imposible acabar con la corrupción de la sonrisa
imposible saber entre tantas mascaras,
nos arroja a todos, silenciosamente al mismo vertedero
allí mismo donde duermen los papeles de la libertad...

Spirit Thom

Wings Weighed Down With Lead

Black & white means more than color
Apartheid -who is armed? Who is the hunter?
When you steal the life of one/you lose your only other
Whether or not there is karma/dead black birds everywhere
Soon the winged ones will wonder whether to walk anywhere
Witness eye one million videos/camera phones
Hunting season undeclared/bodies bleeding everywhere
When the young abused as adults incarcerated
& elders in their nests, ponder justice (lost, @ too high a cost)
Is it fatal force or military madness? Some strange PTSD/training
sessions
That treats all innocent as criminal, and takes all right of appeal.
Conference of the Birds is meditating on murder
Blackbirds must fly, despite fatal weathers.
Do not turn away. This could happen to any body.
Soon no bird dare walk, strut, dance, sing nor even try...
And we are all birds. We came from stars. We fly!

Gabriel H. Sánchez

Blacks Alive

One more day
One more dead man
The crime?
Being black in the wrong place
At the wrong time
The time? Any time
The place? Any place
Any means are fit
If he can't breathe
Squeeze the chokehold tighter
If he runs away shoot him
Eight times in the back
If he has a gun blast him
If he has no gun smoke him
If he cooperates taze him stiff
If he resists kill him dead
Whether he's a doctor or a thug
A professor or a drug lord
It's all the same
Black lives matter
When they seize to be
Blacks alive

Xánath Caraza

Hacia el este

Sublime belleza acuática choca
con los rugidos de una guerra.
pasea por cubierta, Aida,
esta dorada mañana.
Camino azul interminable
hacia el este, disfruta.

La tierra la empieza a rodear,
molinos de viento en maduras colinas.
Torrente de imágenes,
el genocidio la inquieta.
Suspira, Aida, recuerdos
ahogados de flameantes noches eternas.

Niños tatuados de guerra,
fotógrafos sin flash,
muros lastimados,
canción de sordas balas
son los ecos de Mostar,
que Aida encuentra.

En las fosas clandestinas
ya no hay blusas desgarradas,
campos minados respira
en el cielo de Mostar,
y un haz de espuma
persigue la nave en la que va.

Faltan sílabas en las calles.
La esperanza no está perdida.
Manos creyentes
levantan el puente en Mostar.
A pesar de las pérdidas y las balas.
A pesar de la implacable guerra.

Aida reconstruye la escuela.
Forja la nueva generación

donde tres religiones van.
Árboles vacíos en la acera
 y la oquedad en la piedra
contrastan con el anaranjado lugar.

La fuerza de unos
hace que renazca
de entre los escombros la ciudad.
Tenacidad de guerrera
y amor en las manos,
Aida a su casa entra.

La del alma eterna,
mujer sabia de Mostar,
se levanta cada mañana y
entre los cerezos camina.
Les canta en secreto sus penas
oraciones matutinas de paz.

Las níveas flores se expanden
cuando las besa.
Honra a los amigos perdidos.
En voz baja, a manera de rezo,
canta sus nombres
a los veintisiete cerezos enaltecidos.

Su dolor se libera
en las doradas ramas.
Una leve sonrisa se dibuja
en la cara.
Amor desbordado,
sólido hierro como fe.

Sonidos de guerra en la mirada.
Sus ojos irradian firmeza.
Corazón de guerrera,
manos de dama.
Aida camina entre flores blancas y
dulces cerezas cada mañana.

(En el Mar Adriático rumbo a Croacia y en Mostar, Bosnia del 13 al 20 de mayo de 2013)

Toward the East

Translated by Sandra Kingery

Sublime aquatic beauty
collides with the howls of a war.
Strolling on deck, Aida,
this golden morning.
Interminable blue path
toward the east, enjoy.

The earth begins to encircle her,
windmills on mature hills.
Stream of images,
genocide unsettles her.
Sigh, Aida, drowned memories
of eternal blazing nights.

Children tattooed by war,
photographers without flash,
damaged walls,
song of muffled bullets
are the echoes of Mostar
that Aida discovers.

In clandestine graves
there are no longer ripped blouses,
mined fields breathe
in the sky of Mostar,
and specks of foam
pursue the ship that carries her.

Syllables are missing on the streets.
Hope is not lost.
Believing hands
raise the bridge in Mostar.
In spite of the losses and the bullets.
In spite of the relentless war.

Aida rebuilds the school.
She forges the new generation
where three religions go.

Bare trees on the walk
and emptiness on the stone
contrast with the orange-colored locale.

The strength of some
brings rebirth
out of the rubble of the city.
Warrior tenacity
and love in her hands,
Aida enters her home.

Woman of eternal soul,
wise woman of Mostar,
she arises every morning and
strolls among the cherry trees.
She secretly sings them her sorrows
morning prayers of peace.

Snowy flowers expand
When she kisses them.
She honors lost friends.
Softly, as in invocation,
she chants their names
to the twenty-seven exalted cherry trees.

Her pain is freed
on the golden branches.
A slight smile is drawn
on her face.
Brimming love,
solid iron like faith.

Sounds of war in her gaze.
Her eyes radiate firmness.
Heart of a warrior,
hands of a lady.
Aida walks among the white flowers and
sweet cherries every morning.

(On the Adriatic Sea en route to Croatia and Mostar, Bosnia from
May 13 to 20, 2013)

Sarah Rafael García

"Pray for the dead, and fight like hell for the living." -- Mother Jones

The Workers

It happened during Thanksgiving week. Yolanda died by carbon monoxide intoxication, in one of the rich neighborhoods, where she was supposed to treat the Goldstein children for lice so they would be ready to return to school after the gluttonous holiday. Although Yolanda was dismissed from her job at the donut shop a few months back, she couldn't resist the temptation to find a new job to replace her third job, as she had done for the last twenty-four months, replacing a third job for another, constantly juggling time and sleep, just to fill her gas tank, feed her kids and pay her rent without accepting public assistance. She prided herself for not claiming food stamps or visiting the local food pantry. As a lice worker, she kept the same type of clients on the same days of the month, picking up extra appointments and choosing days off based on interview opportunities and the second job schedule.

We all met through the company. It wasn't something we were proud of but we all did what was expected of us. And it was better than the alternatives—parenting their children, cleaning offices at night, or smelling like fried food at the end of the day. We were the ones who checked for lice, we were the ones who inhaled the toxins while the real mothers pretended their children were never the ones to start the contamination at school. They were clean, wore nice clothes, they were rich, "rich kids don't get lice," "rich mothers take care of their children," so people say or maybe just secretly believe. No, no, rich people don't let other rich people know their children have lice. We were the only ones who knew which affluent neighborhoods were infected with the parasites; we were the ones they sent to disinfect the rich people, yet they treated us like parasites too.

Obviously, we know that in Yolanda's youth she was smart and driven and was caught by surprise when she got pregnant during her last year in college, at least that is what she told us over a bus ride before she could afford a car. But at thirty-two as a divorced mother of three kids, to try to afford and succeed, for so many years

96

on her own was exhausting. Mrs. Goldstein wouldn't permit Yolanda's car to remain near her house—such an old client too—she insisted for the car to be towed away, before the neighbors could speculate. Within minutes after discovering the body, Mrs. Goldstein organized for another employee to enter her two-story home in suburbia, while Yolanda waited, very pallid in her car, for the ambulance and tow truck to arrive, and passed the first hour of her death accompanied by strangers who knew nothing of her multiple jobs, cramped apartment across town and three children. When we arrived, to take Yolanda's position with the Goldstein's, she was laid on a stretcher in the street; the medic said they should wait for the coroner and covered her with tarps, so that the passerby's wouldn't get frightened, and to save the cookie-cutter neighborhood from a scandal.

We walked into the Goldstein's house, with Yolanda still visible at a short distance and found Mrs. Goldstein confused by her predicament. She kept exclaiming her worries aloud, "Oh, poor, poor Yolanda, such a great loss. What am I to do?" It was my first time visiting the "New Haven" community. Many of the other lice workers spoke about it, in spite of today, the residents gave good tips—unlike the schools or less affluent neighborhoods—but still our everyday work was tedious and infecting. One of us would become the Goldstein's new lice worker, never mentioning Yolanda, or how she poisoned herself in their neighborhood, forsaking a repeat client, with no regard for her children. Our supervisor, also a worker, introduced us to Mrs. Goldstein, who kept wiping invisible tears from the corners of her eyes and repeating her thoughts, "You will let me know if you need anything for the services? I can send flowers, anything, just let me know what is needed."

When we walked out for some fresh air, after three of the six children were treated, we noticed Yolanda was gone. Police officers surrounded her car, rummaging through her purse and overnight bag she always carried with fresh clothes readily available. Yolanda tried to phone her mother and children before starting a shift; she always said it was important to talk to them even though sometimes she went days without actually making the call. When she did make time, she sat in her car to make the phone call before entering the client's home. Yolanda said her mother was a guardian angel, without her, her children would be staying with strangers or she would have given them up to the state along time ago, just for a chance at a better life. The only time off Yolanda claimed were Sunday mornings, she insisted to be present for church time and treat her family to lunch. Sometimes only the children ate a meal just for the free toy while the two mothers watched them eat. Sometimes Yolanda left immediately after church, claiming she had to go to work in order to eat a real meal and take a stroll in the afternoon sun on her own.

The white police officer waved to us, calling us over to Yolanda's car, we just looked at each other and agreed we had to oblige, as we always do. After jotting down our names and place of employment, the white policeman asked for Yolanda's address and next of kin. Then asked if we knew if she lived in her car or such. We told him of her mother, children and apartment, her usual three jobs, her Sunday ritual and how much we couldn't believe she could've killed herself like Mrs. Goldstein had insinuated. The white policeman never looked us in the eyes. He just kept writing down fragments of our words, saying it was a freakish accident, something about an old car with old car issues, and suicide would have to be ruled out by the coroner at a later time.

Because one of her bags had our company logo embroidered on it—a personified brown louse with red lips wearing a sun hat and lab coat—and appeared to only contain company belongings, the white policeman handed the bag to us, as if returning something that was stolen, again without looking at our faces.

It's not often we have to tell people we are lice workers, or as our company owner and clients refer to us "specialists." Most people don't realize delousing involves more than a shampoo rinse. Almost all situations require handpicking individual eggs and dead lice, washing all clothing and linens in hot water, and spraying and vacuuming carpets and home upholstery. No rich parent ever does any part of the process—that's why they hire us. After all, they do get their money's worth.

Mainly we don't announce our type of work because people often fear we might contaminate them. In some cases, people take a step back and scratch their heads, find a way to stay away from us, as if we are the ones with lice. Often we are told by our clients to hide our bags, just say we are a nurse or pediatrician who makes special house calls, for special clients. Our company provides us with lab coats; Yolanda embroidered her name on hers. She said it made her look more like a specialist and less like an imposter in someone's home. We were all told to dress like we belong in lab coats. In each of our bags they provided mascara, lip-gloss and samples of expensive perfume. Yolanda followed all their tips. We just laughed it off and when we felt like it, we applied our make-up. When we didn't feel like it, we just didn't. Most of us wore our hair in buns, like old librarians or picturesque ballerinas. We weren't allowed to wear hairnets, given that we would look like kitchen help. Yolanda always curled the ends of her hair and pinned it perfectly on one side, she said it made her look sophisticated and when accompanied with her reading glasses, she looked more like a doctor, a doctor who got paid ten dollars an hour for two-hour appointments. She carried curlers in her bag and in between jobs she rolled her hair and slept in her car, we knew her routine well, just from talking to her over the phone when we asked her to cover a shift for us.

We didn't go through Yolanda's bag right away, it just felt unnatural to dig through her belongings before her mother and children even knew she was gone. Being it was two days later and it was Thanksgiving and all, we all gathered like family to mourn her death during a potluck, and that's when we opened her bag. We didn't mean to pry, the journal fell out and opened on it's own when we were divvying up her supplies. It wasn't often someone died and we had a surplus of gloves and combs to share. They only give us one extra set of treatment supplies each month for ourselves, rarely enough to keep our own heads rid of lice. Yolanda used tea tree oil on her scalp and tips of her hair to prevent the little suckers from nesting; she was resourceful like that.

Just like we decided to not turn over the bag from the police to the company, we ventured to read her work journal—in spite of all proper etiquette and processes. The names of her children were etched in pencil and the pages were stained by what could've been tears—yes, we simply disregarded our esteem for the dead and hovered over the notebook, babbling like a heard of sheep. Upon flipping the cover open someone protested, in defense of respecting privacy and what her family might think. Then someone else said, "But she's one of us, we all have a skeleton in the closet and withered dreams." In the end, we all hoped it might say why—

yes, we continued with that—maybe we could find out why she felt compelled to do such a thing, something we've all thought about. Why was she working so much just to give up, what about the children or why did she insist on avoiding public assistance. Why, in the end, she turned to death with no regard for the future. The white policeman told us otherwise, but we just felt like in a neighborhood such as "New Haven" a cover up is better than a suicide, you know, anything to protect the rich. So we just began to read aloud, each of us taking turns. The journal started several months back—some time in late August.

"Today I went to sign up for life insurance. The insurance man-agent was very considerate and found an affordable plan. I left there so happy that I decided to spend a couple dollars on a milk shake. I entered the same diner we went to when in college and that nowadays I never enter, because it reminds me that I could afford more luxuries as a broke student than I can at thirty-two with three jobs. In those days, I never really thought about feeding children, I had grand plans to attend graduate school and maybe someday become one of those fancy professors; in fact I vowed I would never be just a worker or a housewife. I knew education was my ticket out of the working-class, and here, in school, we would make lasting friendships that would lift us far beyond the boundaries of our urban neighborhoods—upward mobility, that's what the professor called it. But it wasn't like that. Who would actually believe in the notion that having sex could change a woman's future? Many of the focused ones stayed there, many went further than we could have predicted at those study-breaks at the diner. Others, we who seemed to have all the promise, we remained in the middle of the road or in my case worse than when I entered the institution, tested by the realities of life, isolated by those who graduated and those who never attended college. I had all the intentions to continue with college, the father of my children did, but somewhere between affording daycare and getting pregnant a second time, we agreed I should take a break, just enough to catch up on our finances. Finally, today I came back to the booth where I once pondered my future and I opened the packet of life insurance documents. I read many unfamiliar words, above my understanding, words only my clients could use in everyday language. Everyone was above me, the customers in suits, the parents of my own children's peers and the college students in the next booth. They didn't see me as once being one of them, or just didn't want to. At the most, they offered a faded smile in my direction, a curious look at a distance. Ignore the woman in the old clothes; smile as if you're almost smiling at her. Between them and me intervened the realities of life. I hid myself in the insurance papers, thought of my children, the ever so sweet cold taste of vanilla on my tongue and forgot all the dreams that paraded past me in all the last twenty years.

Never mind what people think, we have raised our children, we have taken good care of our mothers, we have worked and worked. We weren't too proud to take any job that was willing to hire us. We worked on our hands and knees, we worked at 3am, 4am, and at a quarter to midnight. There had been discipline, perseverance, and devotion to do the right thing. Nothing was ever enough, or are we just expecting more? I contemplated accepting public assistance this morning, like many have suggested but I just couldn't. In college we criticized, judged, scowled at women who had more than one child and 'living off' the taxpayers. But the future now lies in our children; we'll do right by them. We'll make sure they keep their pride. I made my way to the donut shop but not without leaving a tip, after all, the waitress is a worker too.

"I arrived late to work. Five minutes late, five minutes that would only consume time to clock in, put on an apron and count out half of the register drawer. Five minutes in our world equals sixty-seven cents of my eight-dollar-an-hour pay; they fired me over sixty-seven cents! The milkshake was two dollars and sixty cents, plus the dollar tip I left for the waitress, that equals about twenty-seven minutes at work. Our lives are calculated by minute moments of poor decisions. My mother, apart from her love for my children and I, lectures me each time I lose a third job. This time she saw me enter the apartment earlier than expected and we set the dinner table together without speaking any words. She's not the quiet type and often knows more than I think, so she proceeded to speak calmly. Before calling the children from their rooms and homework hour, she asked if it was time to put my pride aside and seek assistance.

That if I didn't need to work a third job, I wouldn't miss my children's daily lives, and her gray years. She continued to remind me how growing up on assistance isn't so bad, 'I too raised children on my own and for the most part y'all turned out alright.' My brother was 'the most part.' He finished college and became some sort of an investor, wearing nice suits everyday, living in Manhattan with his new wife. He deals with money everyday, amounts we can't fathom and when I've asked, he has provided help but I always mail him a check to return the debt, a check he never cashes. I ignored her commentary and called for the children. They ran out of their rooms at the sound of my voice, overjoyed by my presence, the youngest requested a signature and five dollars for the first field trip of the semester, the oldest tells the youngest she'll pack him a lunch and give him two dollars from her piggy bank instead, two dollars she's found by collecting pennies on the street. I remained quiet, trying to save the tears for later. The middle child always remains quiet and observes us all, he hasn't spoken to me in three weeks; I missed his birthday, my mother baked him a chocolate cake with sprinkles, she sent a picture to my phone. We working mothers have it hard; we are sheroes to few and parasites to most. As a lice worker I'm reminded of this every time I meet a new client, they treat us like gentle giants at the door but once we enter their castles we become the louse itself until we are needed again. And everything in life is that: you have to disappear to be somebody.

"Today I write to you from my car, we picked up a school appointment for extra hours of work. I had enough time for a thirty-minute nap between our first job and time to catch up with myself. We have no time for men anymore and we don't need them to give us more babies. We usually don't do the head checks because they are not worth our time, nor do we get tipped. It's not like a seven year old knows he should give us his lunch money or even a compliment, we are feared by most children and their parents. Some parents hire us before the school head checks just to avoid any type of embarrassment, but only if the school actually sends a notice home, most of the rich schools do. We usually take those appointments because often enough if a parent hires us to come to their home it is because they know they need us and if they seem nice enough, I offer to disinfect their home for a better rate than if they would book me directly from the company. But not today, today, we're tormenting children, segregating the haves and have-nots from the general population, like a pipeline to prison but with your white-collar crimes and those from the not so nice neighborhoods. I especially dislike reporting a child that looks like one of our own, could be their mother is one of us, too busy to check her child's head, too busy to read the note in the backpack that provides a warning to do treatment at home, too busy, too busy.

I have to find time to get a third job, doing school appointments doesn't provide me with the extra income for the gas tank or the day old food to take home.

"It's been two months, all I can hear in my mind are the voices saying, 'Yolanda, you better find something, or you're gonna keep dropping weight like it's making you money. You can't go on skipping meals to save a dollar here and there.' At times I also hear my kids talking, especially when I sleep in my car, they keep asking the same questions, 'Momma, why do you work so much? Why do you work so much and we still don't got anything? Momma, stay home with us today, please.' On the way to church, my mother keeps telling me, 'Yolanda this car is no good, the smell gives me a headache. It can't be good for you to sleep in here, day after day. You better keep the ignition off during your naps.' The smell gives me a headache too. But the car also saves me time and makes us money, money to finally afford new shoes for school and stay on time with rent. We hope for something better one day, we hope for the weather to stay good, so I don't have to keep the car on during bad weather days.

"Today Sandrine, Carmen and our supervisor Marta each gave me some leftovers to take home. Together, we will see it through.

"We can't, we won't, we won't let them treat us like this. Sandrine, they paid us less than minimum wage! How is it that they want us to clean their house for less than what it cost to buy a meal for five at a decent restaurant? Don't they know? We've counted the two apples and three pears they forgot to eat at the back of the fridge and we had to throw them out while we ration fruit at home, just to make sure we can pack our kids a snack for school. Don't they realize, we carry their mounds of laundry a total of twenty steps to their fancy washer machine, and compare it to the two blocks our kids have to walk to the laundromat? And then asked us if we cooked? We can't remember the last time we cooked for our own children. I won't! We just have to pick up more appointments checking heads.

"Listen ladies, we work too hard to let them beat us down. How are we supposed to rise up, how are we to teach our children to feel proud like their children do? Day in and day out, we pick the dead lice from their babies' heads, we inhale the toxins, we shower with the chemicals so our babies don't have to smell them as often as we do. We must revisit our plan, we will conquer the world and reclaim or stance, no more of being on our knees. Oh how I wish I could really talk you ladies like these stories I write.

"Sunday after church, I took my kids shopping. I let them choose any item they wanted at the store, yes any item. My mother said I was being foolish, I told her, 'What? Am I to leave this world without putting a smile on their faces at least once in my life?' My mother does not know of the plan, she does not know how we all been talking. But I forgot and slipped some words to her. I'm sure y'all will understand. If only they could walk a day in our shoes, if only!

"I don't understand, Carmen, when you said, 'We are worth more alive than we are dead,' you started the conversation. Why do you pretend with me? When we all talked about a 'farewell' party, Sandra you said you'll bring your potato casserole, Marta, you're bringing your Mama's tamales and I said you could ask my mother to bring her special green beans and bacon. Why do you all keep laughing when I mention my departure?

"The voices came back today. They keep coming to me in my dreams. They tell me how life will be better for my children, how my mother will afford a bigger apartment, how my brother will help my sons become investors, how my daughter will learn from

104

my mistakes. We have to stay on track, we have to pick up as many appointments to keep paying the bills, feeding the kids, gassing the car, we have to make it all look normal, normal as we can be.

"I don't know why those damn lice keep poking fun at me. They jump from one kid to the next, without taking particular interest in race or wealth; they hide well in all of them. But I do as I do, I keep smiling, I keep my hair up on one side, 'Turn your frown upside down Yolanda, we gotta keep up with the Jones' or at least get paid by them.'

"It's been three days, three days since I had a real meal. I'm hungry. The donut shop at least gave me free donuts. They fired me for sixty-seven cents, five minutes in our world equals sixty-seven cents of our eight-dollar-an-hour pay; they fired me over sixty-seven cents! The milkshake was two dollars and sixty cents, plus the dollar tip I left for the waitress, that equals about twenty-seven minutes at work. Our lives are calculated by minute moments of poor decisions. Minute decisions that cost more than sixty-seven cents, they cost us a lifetime. The sweet, cold taste of vanilla on my tongue, mmm, yes, the best moment this past year.

"If only I could wish upon a star and ask for a new life, not for me but solely for my children, and my mother, the children need my mother. They would dress in nicer clothes, go to nicer schools, live in a big home, never ever get lice or ignore the people on the street, my mother would make sure of that. I'll make my own wishes come true, y'all will see, I too can dream.

"My mother promised her green beans and bacon dish for Thanksgiving, she said we don't need the bacon, but then I said, 'How will it be your green beans and bacon dish without bacon?'

"This damn car, this damn car! We all talk about how it helps out but in this cold weather, it's no good. I freshen up before I drive to the client's house. I smell like fumes by the time I drive across town, nothing a little perfume can't cover up but my hair, my hair keeps the scent, we can't smell like we live on the streets. Today I wore a bun.

105

"I picked up a few more overnight shifts and a few more school appointments. I also called my brother in New York today, he asked if I needed money, I said no, I said I was just calling to get his opinion on an investment. He said life insurance is always a good thing and that I should tell my coworkers to do the same. He also said he wasn't coming for Thanksgiving. My mother said that was best.

"Just a little rest, a little rest with some warm air on my face to keep me warm, all will feel better, once I keep the cold air out. We don't have to be at the Goldstein's for another forty minutes, just a little rest to ease my mind."

The pages that followed were empty. We didn't want to think about Yolanda's story but we agreed it sounds like she was talking to us, to all the workers. We all set the table for six—her family had agreed to join us. From here until then, we passed the journal around in silence. We tried to make sense, relate it to any words that could have given her the wrong impression, to some type of misunderstanding. We agreed we wouldn't return Yolanda's journal to the family. At six in the evening the doorbell rang, we couldn't even conceive how to face Yolanda's mother and children. We hoped the mother had never seen the journal, just to ease her pain.

Before we could greet Yolanda's mother, she handed us the green beans and bacon dish. The children made their way to the table; her sons asked about tamales and a potato casserole, they said their mother had mentioned the food we had promised. None of them seemed overwhelmed by grief.

"Sorry for your loss, Yolanda was such a hard worker and a dear friend."

"Thank you, it is heartbreaking for the children, you know. God works in mysterious ways, that's what I keep telling the kids."

"Oh yes."

"Yolanda is now one of those stars up in the sky, it will just take some time to settle into our new lives, we all deserve a little rest."

"Yes, ma'am."

"The children think their mother died dreaming in her sleep…It's been awhile since these kids seen a proper meal, seeing their smiles will be a nice way to remember Yolanda, don't you think? Yolanda always had a plan."

"Ma'am?"

"Oh c'mon ladies, let's all get to tasting this fine food, we all work too hard just to eat."

Michael Verderber

LIBERTAD

(Very dim lights come up on two Mexican immigrants on a train car. They are both very dirtied and have horribly tattered clothes and shoes. Julio is lying face up on the floor. He is barely breathing and barely moving. One would assume he is already dead. Bella is also lying on the floor, she is holding onto a banged up plastic milk jug, half full of water. She is staring at the man. She grabs her flashlight, clicks it on. It doesn't work. She gives a tap with her hand and it comes on. She shines it on Julio. She drags herself tiredly to him. She nudges him and he doesn't move.)

BELLA - Señor? Señor?

(She listens into his mouth for breathing and seems to notice nothing. She gets panicky and returns to her spot to obtain the gallon. She dumps some water on his face. He doesn't respond. Suddenly, he springs up gasping for air, as if drowning. He hastily exhales water from his nose. She jumps back startled.)

BELLA - You're alive!?
JULIO - You trying to kill me?
BELLA - No. No. I'm sorry. I thought you weren't breathing. (Pause. Julio says nothing) Are you ok?
JULIO - Yes. Yes, I'm fine. Now. You got water up my nose. (Julio rubs the water on his face and it smears the dirt on his face to reveal a sad, hardened man.) You...you have water.
BELLA - Yes.
JULIO - Wher-- where's my water? Where's my water?
BELLA - Over there...I think. (Points to a dilapidated jug across the stage. Julio drags himself to the half filled gallon. He begins to chug the water.) Easy, we're not there yet. (He stops drinking)
JULIO - Still!? How long have we been here?
BELLA - What do you mean?
JULIO - How long have we been in the car?
BELLA - Since Wednesday. It's Saturday. I think. The car has been

108

stopped for hours. I think they're inspecting. I heard voices earlier. That's why I woke you up. The voices passed by earlier. But I didn't know if—

JULIO - Americanos?

BELLA - Si.

JULIO - (Suddenly gets more lively) Americanos? Are we across?

BELLA - I don't know. I think so. The smell of urine is getting to me...

JULIO - Where are we? Where are we?

BELLA - I don't know. We've been here a while.

JULIO - What do you mean?

BELLA - At the stop. We've been here for a while.

JULIO - Ugh. I can't remember. How did we get here?

BELLA - Francisco. The coyote, as the Americanos call him.

JULIO - I don't remember any Francs--oh, yes I remember. He's the one that told us to take this train, no? That's all I can remember.

BELLA - Si.

JULIO - And where were we supposed to end up?

BELLA - I cannot remember. Something about a city of royalty.

JULIO - Qué?

BELLA - You know. Kings and queens and stuff.

JULIO - Kingsland! No?

BELLA - No, Kingsville. I think. Does that sound familiar to you, Julio?

JULIO - Yes, something like that. How are we supposed to know when we reached this place?

BELLA - I don't remember. We're supposed to look for some city lights and when the lights fade out, we jump out. There, we meet Olivia at some abandoned building. Some farm just north.

JULIO - I'm worried. This plan isn't well thought out. Francisco should have been more specific. Names. We need names of places. How are we supposed to find anything?

BELLA - I don't know. I guess, we just guess.

JULIO - We're supposed to just guess our way into America? And then San Antonio? How do we find that?

BELLA - (In a harsh whisper) Keep your voice down! You'll give us away!

JULIO - I'm sorry.

BELLA - You shouldn't complain. We're here, aren't we? Is this not America? Is this not what we came for?

JULIO - (Firmly) Yes. (Softening) Yes, it is. (Long pause) I never got your name. I'm Julio, y tu?

BELLA - Bella.

JULIO - I'm so damned hungry. I haven't eaten since Tuesday. No. I brought tamales, but I ate them all. Wednesday, I think. At least the smell keeps my hunger at bay.

BELLA - All my fruit has been ruined by the heat.

JULIO - Yes, it is so hot in here. (Begins to wipe his brow)

BELLA - It could have been worse. We could have left in the summer. Leaving this late in the year means we only have to deal with cold. That won't kill you as fast as the heat will.

JULIO - (Chuckles)

BELLA - That wasn't meant to be funny.

JULIO - No, no. Mi abuelita used to tell me that same thing. "Cold won't kill you as fast as the heat". Mi familia always said that if I wanted to move, do it in the winter. It's a little easier. But you have less time to move in the cold.

BELLA - It doesn't really get cold up here. It's not much different than back home.

JULIO - (Makes a strange facial gesture) It's funny. I didn't think I would say this, but...I miss home.

BELLA - I don't.

JULIO - Really? You don't?

BELLA - Well, I guess I do. I miss my bed and the smell of my house but...when I think of how much easier things can be here in America. I don't look back.

JULIO - Yeah, that's what keeps me going, Bella. Bella, right?

BELLA - Yes. (Long pause)

JULIO - Why are you traveling alone? It's dangerous for a woman to run, let alone a man.

BELLA - Don't worry about me. I had four brothers. I'm like the fifth one.

JULIO - Well, you look strong.

110

BELLA - I am. At least, I'd like to think so.

JULIO - Well, we're both still here, aren't we? Alive and in America!

BELLA - It's frustrating.

JULIO - What is?

BELLA - The fact that we're in America right now. Right this second and we can't get out of this car. We have to wait.

JULIO - It's the impatient Mexicans that get caught. They make a run too soon. They bail out on their pick up and they end up right back home.

BELLA - I don't want that.

JULIO - I don't want that either. I thought that there would be more of us. Here, in the car.

BELLA - That's stupid. And too risky. It's much easier to catch twenty people than two. Twenty people get loud and there's a bigger chance of getting caught versus just two.

JULIO - I guess that's true.

BELLA - It is. That's how all my family got caught about six years ago.

JULIO - No kidding.

BELLA - No.

JULIO - So, what are you after? Why did you leave?

BELLA - That's a stupid question.

JULIO - I know why you left, but, I mean, what are you leaving for? Do you understand?

BELLA - Oh, si. Well, I've heard so much of San Antonio. I heard it's like a haven of opportunities. There are so many businesses, places to see, schools. (hesitates) I want to have children someday and I want to make sure they grow up in a good place, get a good education. I don't want them to end up like me.

JULIO - I know how you feel.

BELLA - I guess, I'm not doing this for me. But for them. (Touches her stomach) When they get here.

JULIO - Do you mean...? You are pregnant now?

BELLA - (Pause) Yes.

JULIO - Bella, that's not good. If you get sick, they will get sick and you could both die.

BELLA - I would rather die now, without a child in the flesh, than to watch my son die before my eyes. I...don't think I could handle that. That's why I knew that it is now or never. Now or never.

JULIO - And where is your husband?

BELLA - I don't have one.

JULIO - Oh.

BELLA - He left me. Well, it was more of a...one night stand. We were friends and things go out of hand one night. (Starting to cry) And here I am. Carrying twins.

JULIO - I'm sorry, I'm a bit confused. You don't look pregnant, no offense. But how do you know you have twins?

BELLA - It runs in my family. Every generation has twins, so I'm pretty sure that's what I got.

JULIO - (Long pause) Let me guess, when he found out you were pregnant he split?

BELLA - No. He doesn't know. (Long pause) But he'll find out when I get to San Antonio.

JULIO - Really? You expect to find him in a city that big?

BELLA - I don't know...I'm just here now...(Sips water) It's hot...so what about you?

JULIO - I, I should have been in San Antonio a long time ago. We, I mean my family, were all leaving at the same time. About a week before we were going to leave, my sister got sick. I mean, I didn't think anything of it at the time, but she got worse and worse. My mother said it was a sign. A bad sign to not go. My sister just got worse and worse and it was hard for her boyfriend to take care of her. My family agreed to not go if I didn't. But I knew that if they stayed, we would never be able to go. It's just one of those things, no?

BELLA - Yes.

JULIO - I packed up like I was leaving with the family. We all loaded up to go, I told the driver to take them without me and he did. I told my family that I would be right back, that I forgot something. I think my wife knew when I kissed her "good luck". She knows a "good bye" kiss when she gets one. Anyway, they took off. About four days later, she called me from San Antonio. She wasn't mad because she knew that I had to stay back for my sister. (Wipes his brow)

BELLA - It's best for the sanctity of the family.

JULIO - Yeah, that's why I tricked them. I felt bad, but I love my wife and I knew she'd understand.

BELLA - If she's a good wife, she'll understand. I remember--

(There is a loud banging outside on the train car. Julio signals Bella to keep quiet and not move. The sound is deafening inside the train. There are a series of five bangs and then silence. Julio signals to Bella to cover their ears. There is a long silence and then five more loud bangs. Silence again. More banging is heard in the distance as the noisemaker has moved onto another car.)

BELLA - (Whispering) Why do they do that?

JULIO - When the officers get lazy and don't want to individually check every cart, they just bang on them.

BELLA - What is that supposed to do?

JULIO - Wake up babies and kids I guess. A lot of families go through here and banging scares little kids into giving away their position.

BELLA - My ears hurt.

JULIO - They are supposed to. How much English do you know?

BELLA - Nothing.

JULIO - Not even a little?

BELLA - Barely a word. That's why I was kind of worried about going.

JULIO - So you couldn't understand what they said?

BELLA - No.

JULIO - They said that the next stop was Kingsville, I think.

BELLA - Really!?

JULIO - Shh! Yes. Bella, we are getting out of here.

BELLA - We're in America!

JULIO - They call this the land of the free.

BELLA - This much I know. I'm not going to be like all those others.

JULIO - What do you mean?

BELLA - I'm not going to get caught. I'm going to work my hardest to make something for myself and my children. And mostly, I'm not

113

going to get caught.

JULIO - That's good. I'm sick of hearing about these lazy Mexicans that go to America and just get by. They live off the government or something. If I wanted to just get by I would have stayed at home. I'm here to make a difference in my life...that's why I admire your motivation. (Starts to lay down and yawns) I'm so tired...

BELLA - You're weak. Relax, rest and I'll wake you on our next stop.

JULIO - You are ok then?

BELLA - Next stop freedom?

JULIO - Next stop home.

(Lights fade out)

[FIN]

Silvia Favaretto

<u>Temporali</u>

Echi di bomba
dai profondi pozzi sotterranei
delle mie interiora.

La paura tremula
ancora sconquassa la mia
carne e il mio respiro.

Quando fuochi artificiali
o frecce tricolori
portano rumore festoso
è solo il dolore antico che si ridesta.

Echi di bomba
dai profondi pozzi sotterranei
delle mie interiora.

<u>Temporales</u>

Ecos de bomba
desde los profundos pozos subterráneos
de mis entrañas.

El miedo trémulo
todavía destroza
mi carne y mi respiración.

Cuando fuegos artificiales
y flechas tricolores
llevan ruido a fiesta

Es sólo el dolor antiguo que se vuelve a despertar.

Ecos de bomba
desde los profundos pozos subterráneos
de mis entrañas.

Non toccatela

A Farkhunda, assassinata a Kabul dai fondamentalisti

"Questo momento mi appartiene
ed io lo regalo a mia madre
che per tutta la vita ha ricamato i suoi desideri
su scampoli di cotone
solo per permettere a mio padre
di soffiarcisi il naso..."
(Basir Ahang)

Non insudiciate il suo corpo d'avorio
Non toccate i suoi capelli d'ebano
Non sgualcite le sue vesti violacee
Non appropriatevi anche della sua tomba
Se giá avete scritto il suo destino
Ora solo noi alzeremo il suo feretro
Solo noi l'accompagneremo nella luce
Solo mani femminili la spalmeranno d'unguenti
E la vestiranno per l'al di lá
Non vi é mai appartenuto il suo corpo
Né la sua vita
Né la sua morte.

No la toquen

A Farkhunda, asesinada en Kabul por los fundamentalistas

"Este momento me pertenece
y se lo regalo a mi madre
que durante toda su vida ha bordado sus deseos
sobre retazos de algodón
sólo para permitirle a mi padre
sonarse en ellos la nariz.."
(Basir Ahang)

No ensucien su cuerpo de marfil
No toquen su pelo de ébano
No chafen su ropa morada

No se adueñen también de su tumba
Si ya han escrito su destino
Ahora sólo nosotras levantaremos su ataúd
Sólo nosotras la acompañaremos en la luz
Sólo manos femeninas la untarán de ungüentos
y la vestirán para el más allá
Nunca les perteneció a ustedes su cuerpo
Ni su vida
Ni su muerte.

Dustin Pickering

Texas King

You have poisoned the water well
and let poverty rule the border.
Why are you the King?

You discipline me with the lash
when I ask questions.
Do I say with my eyes,
"Make me the whipping boy?"
Why again are you the King?

I am beaten for asking for bread;
I am drowned for asking for water.
Why can't my legacy be realized
in this country of drunken stupidity?
Why are you the King?

I am punished for another child's distress—
I am the scapegoat, the salvation,
for a tradition of King's lies.

Francisco X. Alarcón

WHAT IS RACE?

what is race?
but a precious gift
bestowed to all of us

by our common
primordial mother
in ancestral Africa

we, her children,
went on to populate
all continents

we, as colorful birds,
turned to different
skin colors and tones

but we all remained one
as branches of the same
ancient baobab tree

what is race?
but a dream, colorful
as a rainbow

a fantasy used
by some to impose
a nightmare on others

empires expanded,
conquered new lands;
their policies were

to divide, chain,
slave, denigrate
native peoples

in order to impose
an oppressive
social caste system

what is race?
but a bound
for resistance

a call to struggle
for liberation
against racism

what is race?
it's not a question
but an assertion

of an invention
since there is just
one true race

one human race.
a product of love:
the cosmic race!

¿QUÉ ES RAZA?

¿qué es raza?
sino un precioso don,
regalo de nuestra

madre primordial
de todos los pueblos
de Africa ancestral

nosotros, sus críos,
nos fuimos a poblar
todos los continentes

como aves multicolores
nos volvimos diferentes
en tono y color de piel

pero seguimos siendo uno
como ramas del mismo
árbol baobab milenario

¿qué es raza?
sino un sueño colorido
como el arco iris

una fantasía usada
por unos para imponer
una pesadilla a otros

imperios se expandieron,
conquistaron tierras;
sus políticas fueron

dividir, encadenar
esclavizar, denigrar
a pueblos nativos

para imponer
un opresivo sistema
social de castas

¿qué es raza?
sino un amarre
para la resistencia

una llamada a luchar
para la liberación
contra el racismo

¿qué es raza?
no es una pregunta
sino una afirmación

de una invención
ya que en realidad
solo hay una raza

una raza humana,
un producto del amor:
¡la raza cósmica!

Anita Menegozzo

Sterpaglia

Sterpaglia
che aggrappa
E che mi trattiene
ogni passo
ogni gamba
E appende alla veste
Arrestati
Ascoltami
Arresta!
Mi grida la terra
da sotto me stessa
Io so come è andata
Mi soffia
Li tengo in ben più di quaranta
Qui già tra le braccia
Mi inciampa
mi intralcia il cammino
Denuncia! Protesta !
Intona qualcosa
che faccia notizia
Mi prega
Finché non le cedo
ambedue le ginocchia
Finché le mie unghie
non pianto nell' erba
Finché non tempesto
di poveri pugni
il mondo che tace
e la sua indifferenza
Finché non la scavo
convulsa
frugando ogni zolla
Finché la mia mano
non stringe la mano
a un giovane grumo di ossa.

Maleza

Maleza
que se enreda
y me detiene
cada paso
cada pierna
y se cuelga al traje
Detente
Escúchame
¡Detente!
Me grita la tierra
desde abajo de mi misma
Yo sé cómo fue
Me sopla
Los guardo a más que cuarenta
Aquí entre mis brazos ya
Me tropieza
me obstaculiza el camino
Denuncia! Protesta !
Declama algo
que cree noticia
Me ruega
Hasta que flaquean
las dos rodillas
Hasta que mis uñas
se clavan en la yerba
Hasta que lleno
de pobres puñetazos
al mundo que calla
y su indiferencia
Hasta excavar
convulsa
hurgando cada terrón
hasta que mi mano
estrecha la mano
a un joven grumo de huesos.

Baljeet Singh

I wish I could call 911 for help
I heard my nanny
Screaming out of
The deadly attack
I was crying hard
While she dashed out to see
The scene
Leaving me alone at my home
Watching from my windowpane
Thick diabolic black smoke far away
Engulfing:
Roads, houses, buildings,
Skedaddling people
NYC.
The body was scorched
And bruised badly,
Half of the head
And a hand missing
Jellified blood under her torn skirt
Stopped seeping through
Her genitalia
Her white milky thighs
Were squalid like of beggars
I was afraid
Of that one eyed ugly lady
Whose terrible dead eye
Stared at me
They said she was my mother
But only I know
How beautiful was my mommy!
One day I will grow up
I will pamper all hate in me
But I won't seek revenge
As forgiveness is the key
I won't burn their houses,
Or see their children crying
Over dead bodies
Like I cried over
A half dead body.

Part III

"THE MEMORY OF OPPRESSED PEOPLE IS ONE THING THAT CANNOT BE TAKEN AWAY, AND FOR SUCH PEOPLE, WITH SUCH MEMORIES, REVOLT IS ALWAYS AN INCH BELOW THE SURFACE."

— HOWARD ZINN

Nephtalí De León

<u>America, America,</u>
   <u>You Hear the Tolling Bell?</u>
         (screaming storm! monsoon rain!
            I'm on the road once again)

I'm splitting from the wild borderlands
I said goodbye to Donna, Ramón, y la Fran
wheels heading north, checkpoints everywhere
airplanes, helicopters, mounted police
gadgets, sirens, flashing in the air
what's going on? Gestapos everywhere!

2nd time I'm stopped, where were you born?
what you got in there? open your van!
painting of the Virgin, what's that in her hand?
she's my freedom torch-- cause I aint no slave
Lord! I got away! -- did I see someone wave?

stupid! keep on driving, don't you stop!
my heart is throbbing atomic clock
all I can think of is migra attack,
the Virgin she whispers "you gotta go back!"

thunder and lightning nature is a freak
two little somethings pop out of the weeds
two mangy wet dogs starving and weak!
shaking and a'trembling they limp into my van

step on the gas or they'll throw you in the can
I share my hot coffee liberate my tacos
hey! eat 'em kinda slow or you're gonna gag
they wolf 'em down quick! and almost ate the bag!
had no food for days, scratched from head to toe

where you coming from? where you going to?
whimpering sounds, "17 of us, we both got away!"
kidnapped by the Zetas, criminal gangs,
machine guns full -- hand grenades

125

turned into their hands by immigration goons
immigration creeps on the Mexican side
inhuman traffic, you're guessing what's up
they got their mordida they got their cut!

ransom paid, a thousand dollars each
plus $5 thousand dollars, robbery fee,
underground railroads, American gangs
damned "coyotes" treat people like ghosts
non-human beings, cannot think or feel
leave 'em anywhere for all their bones to rot
they sleep out in the wild in a ditch for a cot!

mud-caked zombies in my back seat curled
I could barely tell they were two young girls
matted hair, wet soaking jeans, nasty tennis shoes
wonder if they're human – these 2 alien things --
young warrior girls, from Honduras, Salvador,
trekking toward Maryland, and also New York
how did they get here, these diminutive things?
must be flying angels — I see their broken wings…!

"I never met my father" said the youngest one
he was killed in the wars I only have my mom
today is my birthday I wish she was here
when did you last see her, remember do you know?
I was 9 when she kissed me, crying went away
that was 10 years ago, I'm 19 years today

equally small, but much older was the other
had left 3 children in care of her mother
had not seen her husband in more than 4 years
their watery eyes showed their sacrifice and fears
their souls were a'melting like pieces of ice
the old one from Honduras, she was 25!

I leave 'em alone and return where we stopped
with a sweet creamy cake strawberries on top
we found a large tree and the sky for a dome
3 brown colored gypsies raised a birthday song
to a dead tired elfin so far away from home!

make another food stop! there's only hot dogs
their mouths are so dry they aint got no spittle
they later reported on a long distance call
they ate and they tried a cross-cultural riddle --
"some bread with a meat in the middle!"

several hours later we get to my home
a little more at ease if hurting all along
quick! make a call -- Chicano connection!
Chino , Antonio, Regina and María
Dallas, Houston, Washington D.C.
the migra's got the guns and the high-tech gear
but we got so much power they will never see
not in their life time or a hundred years!

there's a spirit in our bodies, ancient like a soul
nothing can destroy it, it has no shape or form
ancestral power, we get it when we're born
we're made of mist and myth -- a legendary race
you kill one of us, two will take our place!

everyone has failed to erase us from our land
migra, genocide, -- the wall planned in hell
they're all doomed to fail, evil always fell
America, America, you hear the tolling bell?

Planeta de Gorilas

(translated from original in Spanish)

I saw through the window one day
that the time of the apes,
    the century of gorillas,
    the brave new world, and 1984.
    were already complete.

I saw a black man with a rifle,
a Chicano with two guns,
I saw a native of Aztlan
    (eyes full of water and caiman
    his sandals were both full of mud)
    there was distance in his footsteps
    he had some fish in his hat –
    as if in crossing a river.
He was loaded with highways and customs
bridges of malice and perfidy,
with a face full of madness he rushed
to the clutches and fries of McDonalds
demanding in honkyfied English
the latest hamburger shit-food

In a corner forgot in my mind
    an Indian was chained to a skyscraper
    (of silver and bills were the chains)
    like ancient Prometheus
    a much deeper red was the carpet
    and much brighter bright was the suit
    worn by the red skin
    que la antigua pintura de su cuaco

I saw the plan of unchecked control
    was tightening its chains
    amidst the tribes
    of oppressed people

Other giveaway human fools
    (the hour of turncoats is over,

128

who'd want to buy a puppet and an asshole)
    packing deadly weapons
    using point blank
    inhuman technology of rape
    – a power temporarily bestowed

I saw the invasion of apes
    oppressing their very own kind
    (disgusting and sick
    are the jerks of the world!)

But now even now
in the planet of the Apes
even now in the hour of sorrow;
.. .not all those in positions
    have become our foes,
    nor all those with a rifle in their hands
    can we call our friends…

<u>Planet of the Apes</u>

YO VÍ POR LA VENTANA UN DÍA
QUE LA ETAPA DE MONOS,
EL SIGLO DE GORILAS,
EL BRAVE NEW WORLD, Y 1984
ESTABAN YA COMPLETO

Ed O'Casey

Dinner in Juárez

there must be

       gods

     in contention here

     cardboard
       schools   coke-stained

  dollars   Santa Muerte

          her
             strokes

          of blood

     narcos   the
        real
        prophets

messages   written in dismemberment

   the worst orphanage

     its waiting list

Conceal and Carry

I could buy dozens of guns
　　　　because of my record

　　　　　　fill my trunk with an arsenal

　　　　　　quadruple what I spent

　　　it is near impossible to buy guns in Mexico

desperation best operates inside

the proposal:

　　stock the kitchen
　　dress my girl

　　　　　　bear　　　　　　the report
　　of a body found　riddled and strung
　　drowned　　in border business

Juan Carlos Castrillón

A Poem For Ayotzinapa And Ferguson

And it happened that the daughters of Earth gave birth to men:
archers, gladiators, sick platoons of little butchers.
The world was considered a natural despoilment, organic evolution
of the soul on the human knees.
And those sad beasts grew up to turn into a plague for themselves.
And Earth was dried, blinded, hardened by the sweat of suffering.
And the last poets took out their eyes, and chained their ears to
unlearn the screaming.
And the fists of the unworked got tangled up with surgical hatred
against their comrades.
And the races of the planet gathered to demand Lazarus to expire, to
be saved.
And the sky long time ago has dried into a suicidal scab.
And the left ventricle is a brothel of extenuated reptiles.
And the placentas are stabbed everyday in the canibal market.
And the hormone of hate increased until it became a thinking cell.
And it devoured its clone in the ovule of time.
And devastated every flesh on the face of the Earth.

Canción del despertar

El corazón es una chispa
de necios veredictos
La calavera es una urna
de expertas contradicciones
La rosa es una cita
de pétalos confusos
La sangre es el flujo
cosificante de la historia
La luna es el polo
extasiado de la espera

Sobre el cráneo de la aurora
enmudecen las tribunas

El reloj es un molusco
carcomido por la estepa
La niebla es el caracol
sagrado de la guerra
Los rayos del sol
son los dispensadores arrepentidos
de la cruel esperanza
El fuego es el vivificador
molecular de nuestro espíritu
La mariposa es la cómplice
virtual de la volatibilidad
en la sorpresa del genoma
La guitarra es la evolución constante
de todas las especies vegetales
La espuma es el labio
insaciable de la ola
El ritmo es el demoledor
ancestral de lo intocable
La voz de la mujer es el aglutinador
biológico de la materia
La telaraña es la catedral voraz
de los puntos cardinales
La rabia es el detonador
infinitesimal de las dendritas
El semen es la baba del cosmos

enardecida en nuestros tercos testículos
La saliva es la florescencia
amniótica en la salinidad de los océanos

La voluntad acelera el destino de los astros

Que la enunciación llegue
hasta la conciencia
No estoy
por depositar
mi error
en su persona
Que la luz nutra
la nobleza de la psique
Que la vida crezca
hasta inundar el cielo
Que la mañana desflore.

Abigail Carl-Klassen

Recidivism is just

a long ass word and
adjudication means you can't
read this. Sixteen, can't read shit,
left on the walls after you tried
to eat your own shit. To say fuck
them. But then, they stuck
your ass in "hotel," solitary, how
you like it there? Is it like smoking
blunts and breaking probation? Swiping
40s from the 7-11 and masturbating
in the park? Is it like exposing
yourself to substitute teachers,
or is it more like clubbing
those faggots down at the Old
Plantation? Bat, black with blood
as you ran, like a little pussy, but not
fast enough? Or, is it like bitch
slapping your grandma, then finding
out that every gangsta on the block
wants to smash your face. On the curb
teeth first, because they love
their mamas and hate little white
boys facing adjudication for fucking
their sisters? Just wait until you are old
enough. You better watch your ass
out in population at Huntsville Prison.

Repeat Offender: Under the Freeway Murals, Lincoln Park, El Paso, Texas

Take that eyebrow pencil away from that girl
in the Oakland Raiders jacket. With her ear
holes pulled open by fake silver hoops, a smack,
tat against her neck. And she's about to tell some
bitch to get up out of her business. You know
that you should take it, by the way she drags
her black, week-old press on nails into the back
of that kid in the sideways cap. With his Dickies
hanging off his ass down to his work boots. She
hooked him up in a temporary position with
Southwest Staffing Solutions. Where people are
our business. Part-time. And he works with power
drills, spray paints, paint brushes, but no safety
glasses. He doesn't take them home, though,
to show his cousin with the Kool-Aid moustache,
because he knows. That he would show Chapo
how to hold the can in his hand. With his finger
on the trigger. And blow the brains out
of everybody that says he's good for nothing
but jail. Oye, this arte is not beautiful, it throws
up and bleeds. Broken teeth, dirty needles, spent
condoms, and tall boys with bullet holes: under
overpass bridges, crack houses, the back door
of Family Dollar, and on the front of Early Head
Start. And everywhere else white walls get
jumped because they just aren't tough enough.

Silvia Mar

Al pueblo que aún no está acabado

¿Y si dejamos de evadir la realidad?
¿Y si dejamos de anudarnos en una cópula de quimeras?
-Y no es que las quimeras sean malas-.
¿Y si dejamos de ser manada de borregos amaestrados?
¿Y si dejamos de revolcarnos en un chiquero?
¿Y si dejamos de comportarnos como los cerdos?
¿Y si a la fuerza pública la enclaustramos en fosas?
¿Y si mejor la incineramos?
¿Y si a la libertad de los asesinos la emboscamos?
¿Y si dejamos de pagarles a los diputados perezosos?
¿Y si estrangulamos las riquezas de empresas extranjeras?
¿Y si reformamos las reformas que nos han empobrecido?
¿Y si pujamos y empujamos?
¿Y si soltamos y caminamos?
¿Y si mejor corremos?
¿Y si nos apresuramos a esclavizar la impunidad?
¿Y si a nuestra ignorancia le ponemos fin?
¿Y si al amor lo convertimos en revolución?
¿Y si revolucionamos al amor?
¿Y si revolucionamos al amor?
¿Y si revolucionamos al amor?
¿Y si…?

<u>Oremos…</u>

Por los 43 que bajaron al abismo y bebieron de cálices amargos.
Por los 43 que comieron de las sombras
sangre de angustia derramada.
Por los 43, cuyos rostros se quemaron arrancados de la vida
y sus manos las ataron.
Por los 43 que no se han ido, ni los han desaparecido
porque han resurgido de las fosas entre el aullido de los lobos.
Porque han resurgido del azufre y de las llamas.
Porque la magia ha resurgido de la muerte
y está por doquier:
en el amanecer, los maizales y en las ramas,
en el caminar de los que manifiestan…
Oremos…
Por los 43 que han sido canto,
un canto de pasos que hoy no lloran.
Porque hemos de morir para que su lucha siga viva
y su espíritu guerrero no se pierda en las quimeras
y coman el pan del cielo y la espiga de su suelo.
Para que emerjan sus rostros de las flores…
Oremos.

Anna Betts

From the Shadows of the Auction Block:
Ferguson

Tonight I need shit with a beat-to match the pounding pulse of this piece of our universe loosing its fucking mind.

Masked, storming mobs, burning, shattering, slashing-a tangible symbol of our unimaginable rage.

Not again-a collective cry unheard, above the roar of pain for the loss of a life just flipping the page.

A mothers scream for a first born son, a father's anguish of promise gone.

Now I need a rhythm to rattle my teeth

To cover my nerves raised in surrender

Tonight I turn up the volume trying to drown out the sound of my heart breaking.

To somehow stop a flood of tears if I allowed myself to fall into the darkness of this night.

As our collective moan ignites an unseen fear growing thick enough to taste.

Anger pounding now across a nation glued to networks, tweets, posting-comments; only questions form, then swirl into our dirty waters.

The beat of our nation pulses, throbs with a sound many hoped had at least been muffled.

But tonight it screams in smoke, tanks, snipers-streams live.

Fall now and the world waits in fear or its anticipation.

As the world waits, the beat and rhythm of fear becomes almost a life of its own.

A shape emerging from the shadows-our shadows of anger and pain

Something new yet not we've just given it a jolt

Our palpable electricity releasing months, decades, centuries of unanswered rage.

The world watches media networks, updates, in this time of right now, a few things get lost-glossed over; pieces of a truth we may never know.

And we wait, the pounding of our hearts ready to burst, soon releas ing the muted roar across cities.

Done with madness and other shit that doesn't make sense, screaming enough of snap decisions long held assumptions resulting in another son gone.

In the days of a sudden winter, we prepare ourselves to charge through layers of fleeting comfort, for a sound to pull the caps off-will anyone be listening?

In this sudden winter, things feel miles away from that moment in history, wiped out by the evil we never addressed.

Oh yes, debated, legislated, convened, reams spilled over wounds never healed.

The world waits, days before the start of another holiday season

Peace joy and good will to all

We wait

The world watches-will anyone listen?

And the 12 have spoken.

Closures and recalls, my heart pounds, to the beat of disbelief, flipping through bits and bites of opinion and fact, mind spinning with things that might or might not set off

It's the unknown chasm widening before the silence, pounding with each passing hour.

And it is done, not shocked but saddened, as I fight back tears, the monster lives.

Here's the world on fire, our collective cry

Another black face occupying a space among others, gone at the hand behind a badge and gun.

Us coming out of the shadows of the auction block, refusing to go back

Demanding to be seen, and heard, recognized

Not just categorized

Go beyond our colored faces; wait before deciding automatically that we're all up to no good

Here's the world lit up

Bright orange flames across the darkness

A symbol of our rage released

Uncovering all of our jagged oozing sores.

Antonella Barina

<u>Hanno condannato a morte i re magi</u>
10 agosto 2014
Per gli Zoroastriani d'Iraq

Hanno condannato a morte i Re Magi
Manca un solo giorno allo sterminio
del Popolo delle Stelle
Dov'è il Dio unico che ama
tutti gli uomini e le donne?
Il Dio giusto che promette il Paradiso?
Il Dio dei Presepi con gli agnelli umili
che brucano tra le palme?
Dio, se il Popolo delle Stelle
sarà cancellato da questa terra
autorizza il mare a varcare i confini
Non vi sono piedi degni di calcarla
Scendi a difendere gli Yazidi
che non hanno né Papa né Imam né Rabbini
ma hanno l'eleganza di chi balla
sotto la volta del cielo stellato
Luna e sole tra le mani
La danza da cui nascono i pianeti
Vieni, Sole, a far da scudo
a chi non ha soldi per comprare le armi
Vieni, immacolata incalpestata Luna
con la forza delle maree
a fermare gli assassini
Stormi di avvoltoi già aspettano
I corpi consegnati all'aria
- Akbaba, l'avvoltoio
le grandi ali della morte
Akbaba, il transito verso altri mondi -
mentre qui da noi
spariscono i passeri

Sentenciaron de muerte a los reyes magos
10 de agosto 2014
Para los Zoroastrianos de Irak

Condenaron a muerte a los Reyes Magos
Falta sólo un día para el exterminio
del Pueblo de las Estrellas
¿Dónde está el Dios que ama
a todos los hombres y a las mujeres?
¿El Dios justo que promete el Paraíso?
¿El Dios de los pesebres con corderos humildes
que pacen entre las palmas?
Dios, si el Pueblo de las Estrellas
será eliminado de esta tierra
autoriza la mar a cruzar las fronteras
No hay pies dignos de pisarla
Baja a defender los Yazidos
que no tienen ni Papa ni Imam ni Rabinos
pero tienen la elegancia de los que bailan
bajo la bóveda del cielo estrellado
Luna y sol en sus manos
La danza que creó los planetas
Ven, Sol, como escudo
Para los que no tienen dinero para comprar armas
Ven, inmaculada inhollada Luna
con la fuerza de las mareas
para parar los asesinos
Bandadas de buitres ya esperan
los cuerpos entregados al aire
- Akbaba, el buitre
las grandes alas de la muerte
Akbaba, el tránsito a otros mundos -
mientras aquí cerca de nosotros
desapareceran los gorriones

henry 7. reneau, jr.

freedomland blues

all wars begin long before the first shot is fired & continue
long after the last bullet has done its job.

think, biological aversion: every dark-skinned outlier a shade of
Spade
that buries humanity beneath the semantics of language, beneath
the half made song of immigrant crows, accents
not deemed Amerikkkan enough
as refugees walk into the unknown, seeking the edges of indifferent
power
with only blind hope balanced on their heads,

        not unlike a stone ax crushing a baby's skull
    is no different from a Hellfire missile, except in its efficiency for
                collateral damage.

our political correct, a vestigial tail of greed, hypocrisy &
devil-hate,
delineating them/those "Others" running from 3rd world tyranny to
Amerikkkan terrorism—
from demeaning labels Made in Amerikkka, corporate-shadow cabals
&
blind-mouth, eyes-shut-wide "guest expert" propaganda—
preening Amerikkkan Idol one-hit-wonders & skank-on-fame celebri-
ho's
who flash mononymity, conflict diamonds & famous-for-being-
famous like a handful
of hurt consecrating the names of 500,000 murdered Muslims per
gallon of gas.

    think, bugs in velvet-lined boxes, horizon to horizon across foreign,
                desert sand,
        an occupation with imperialism, by Predator drone &
           red, whiter, blue(s) as the screaming child
    running through a mine field, trying to dodge the wrath of Jim
                Crow's Christian God,
                her amputated stump
    a talisman, rebuking recycled Viet Nam in Iraq & Afghanistan.

our Manifest Destiny, a prestidigitated devil-mocracy,
is the P.R. story of little tin gods with guns & ammo, a retribution in
context
with post-Cold War hysteria,
reinvented War.   On.   Terror.   post-9/11 threat-level paranoia:
surrounded by Muslim terrorists in suicide vests & cyber-terrorists
inciting gigabyte-sized alarm in Internet increments; if you phone
Obama
& tell him to fuck himself terrorist threat & deaf, dumb & blind-
leading-blind domestic terrorism: a homegrown insanity
designing fertilizer IEDs, shooting sprees & the hate that made hate
a political correct N-word this & bitch, ho', skeeza that.

here, a thug nigga', stereotyped "suspicious" with Skittles in his
pocket,
saggin' & his hoodie hung,
there, a goddamn faggot castrated by Bible-thumper hypocrisy,
he/she/them there/those indigenous, illegal aliens become
graffiti-ied slurs on "Safe Zone" walls & the hangman noose in the
university quad.

CNN ticker-tape sound-bites that deceive distort & deny,
designating new niggers we should be very afraid of.   & we are
the unlucky ones,

saved from nuclear-stalemate propaganda to drown in nuclear-winter
oil
restrained behind police-state lines, razor wire & cyclone fence,
phone tap GPS & national security duct tape of activist dissent—
body scanners, yellow caution tape & sexual assault at the TSA
security gate—

it's like we've fallen & we cain't get up;

not unlike Occupy Amerikkka we shall overcome . . . someday,
is a dangerous phrase for never, strangled in the "Jesus wept"
cowardice
of non-violent dissent, where every po-po's predatory promiscuity
portends a pig
named Pike who pepper-sprays peaceful protesters—& Jesus on the
cross

with turn the other cheek,

gets slapped twice—
not unlike enemy combatants, bagged, bound & gagged, awaiting
an unknown fate; no one is coming to rescue them,
the freedom fighters dying nameless—abandoned by our cowardice
& the reflective

shame of apathy;
a freedomland dichotomy,
but some will never live to beg, in collective fear,   of Homeland
Insecurity.

Giorgia Pollastri

<u>Tel Al zaatar (tra Siria e Palestina)</u>

Profumava di timo la collina
quando mia madre
raccoglieva le piccole foglie
ascoltando le nostre risate.

Il sole splendeva mentre nell'acqua
sul fuoco ancora bollivano le foglie.
...
Ancor più si spandeva il profumo
quel giorno ...

ed il sangue scorreva sulla collina
dove il verde arrossava
e il dolore cresceva

e la mamma
cercava i suoi figli
e la mamma
non vedeva più il sole.

Torneranno i tempi del profumo di timo?
Nel silenzio del cuore
la mente ancora sogna.

Tel Al zaatar (entre Siria y Palestina)

Perfumaba de tomillo la colina
cuando mi madre
recogía pequeñas hojas
escuchando nuestras risas.

El sol resplandecía mientras en el agua
sobre los fuegos todavía hervían las hojas.
...
Aún más esparcía el aroma
ese día ...

y la sangre corría en la colina
donde el verde se enrojecía
y el dolor crecía

y la madre
buscaba a sus hijos
y la madre
no veía más el sol.

¿Regresarán los tiempos del aroma del tomillo?
En el silencio del corazón
la mente todavía sueña.

Sarah Frances Moran

You Can't Eat Money

You can't eat money
and you can't base
every principle you care for
on the benjamins...

they don't care for you
they won't hold you
and they destroy
everything

when everything is ash
when there's just a wasteland
will the vote you cast
protecting your dollar
mean anything?

After all the rights are gone
After the idea of loving yourself is made illegal
After they finally win the war
and you realize you were a pawn...
will you then realize how it didn't matter?

The dollar won't bring you to peace
and you're blind to the economic apocalypse that your ideology is
harboring

When people starve so we can fuel SUVs
When children are sent away to be murdered and raped so we don't
have to feed them
When teenagers kill themselves because your economic vote also
meant negating their lifestyle
When raped women die aborting babies in illegal backdoor clinics
When racism continues to run rampant through city streets

When you tell me,
you love everyone
you have gay friends
you have no qualms over immigration
you want to see the world a non-racist place

you appreciate a woman's body
but you just can't vote to give away your money

that's when you've failed

Your failure
I promise you
won't ever be judged by what the ATM spits at you

It's going to be judged by the lives you turned your eyes on
so that you could look to the artificial lights of Bank of America

It's going to be judged on your myopic indifference
and by your inability, to eat money.

Lucia Guidorizzi

Verso il centro della ferita

14 Marzo 2008 : A Lhasa, in Tibet, l'esercito cinese reprime nel sangue
una manifestazione di monaci buddisti tibetani, che manifestavano
nel giorno del 49° anniversario dell'occupazione cinese in Tibet.

L'unico modo possibile superare la violenza subita è riconoscerla,
chiamarla per nome e camminarci dentro

Mi dirigo al centro della ferita
ne riconosco la notte
affacciandomi alla finestra
interna e silenziosa
del non detto
percepisco l'abisso
in cui si agitano
i demoni insonni
della storia

Prendo in consegna il trauma
me ne faccio carico
sto in questa emozione incancellabile
e solo abitandola mi libero dalla sua presa

Tocco e chiamo per nome la ferita
la evoco davanti ai miei occhi
il dolore cambia senza sosta
è vibrante sorprendente vivo

Osservo l'albero bruciato dal fulmine
vedo cadere tutte le sue foglie
ne riconosco lo strazio insostenibile
ascolto cosa ha da dirmi

Sto al centro della notte
che sanguina

Hanno ucciso hanno negato
hanno taciuto
e fanno finta di niente

Ma quelle ombre di sangue parlano
della violenza che tiene in scacco un paese
Le montagne hanno visto le montagne sanno e riconoscono l'abuso

Solo raccogliendo il lamento
inascoltato dei morti
si possono trovare parole
che sciogliendo il maleficio
siano in grado di illuminare
il futuro

Hacia el centro de la herida

14 de Marzo 2008 : En Lhasa, en Tibet, el ejercito chino reprime en la sangre una manifestación de los monjes budistas tibetanos, que se manifestaban en el día del 49º aniversario de la ocupación china en Tibet.

La única forma posible para ir más allá de la violencia sufrida es reconocerla, llamarla por su nombre y caminar adentro de ella

Camino hacia el centro de la herida
reconozco en ella la noche
asomandome a la ventana
interior y silenciosa
de lo no dicho
percibo el abismo
en el que se mueven
demonios en vela
de la historia

Tomo en depósito el trauma
me hago cargo de ello
estoy en esta imborrable emoción
y sólo habitándola me libero de su agarre

Toco y llamo con su nombre la herida
la evoco delante de mis ojos
el dolor cambia sin descanso
es vibrante sorpresivo vivo

Observo el árbol quemado por el rayo
veo caer todas sus hojas
reconozco su suplicio insostenible
escucho lo que tiene para decirme

Estoy en el centro de la noche
que sangra

Han matado han negado
han callado
y disimulan

Pero aquellas sombras de sangre hablan
de la violencia que tiene en jaque un país
Las montañas vieron, las montañas saben y reconocen el abuso

S'olo recogiendo el lamento
desatendido de los muertos
se pueden encontrar palabras
que desatando el maleficio
sepan inluminar
el futuro

Ofelia Faz-Garza

9/11 Induced Psychosis

Country has been living in a perpetual state of
    disbelief,
        indignation,
            paranoia
                stagnation

Talking heads telling me, telling you, telling us
be afraid,
they're coming
them, those people
they gonna get you

Boogey men…women…children
Hatred for anyone who
    Looks,
        Sounds,
            Dances,
                Thinks differently

Forgetting the others are
Mothers, fathers, friends
Forgetting we share a space,
Breathe the same air
Love the same way
Forgetting, forgetting, forgetting
I am you
they are us,
we are them

Cinzia Marulli

<u>Gaza 2014</u>

Quella piccola carne bianca
che giace santa tra le macerie
è l'anima di tutti noi
che scaviamo tra le mura
frantumate della pazzia

Santa Santa Santa è la Terra
che ti accoglie
figlio del nostro grembo
noi madri urliamo
il travaglio oscuro della tua morte

Bevi
piccolo innocente cadavere
Bevi
il latte del nostro seno
bevilo
mentre noi piangiamo
i nostri peccati.

Gaza 2014

Esa pequeña carne blanca
que yace santa debajo de los escombros
es el alma de todos nosotros
que excavamos entre las paredes
trituradas de la locura

Santa Santa Santa es la Tierra
que te recibe
hijo de nuestro regazo
las madres gritamos
los oscuros dolores de tu muerte

Bebe
pequeño inocente cadáver
Bebe
la leche de nuestros pechos
bébela
mientras lloramos
nuestros pecados.

David Hale

The Color of Bone

Bleached
Not white
But bereft of color

Beyond flesh's tone
One finds all blood is red
The color of unity
Spilled in anger
Hatred or ignorance
Incongruent
To the reality of similarity

Division

It's a problem of history
In acknowledgement of past
The present is segregated

When the price of history
Is more valuable
Than the value of present
We see "American"
As a brand
Like clothing
Not as a bond
Like steel
Welding us together
Armor plates
Protecting each other's lives

Mina Gligorić

<u>Saturación</u>

Vivo en la selva
de colores deslumbrantes
de almas enredadas
El esmalte se agrieta
bajo el triste peso
de deseos no sembrados
La sed es grande
Ahora veo:
para aquellos en el otro lado
sólo alguna cara aquí
brilla con el propósito original
en colores de neón
Todas las demás bailan
en estertor agónico
de atención nunca
prestada
Susurra ambición enferma
se arrancan los rostros
en el cocito de sueños fallados
Abalea la nieve

Сатурација

Живим у џунгли
заслепљујућих боја
запетљаних душа
Глеђ пуца под тужним теретом
недосејаних жеља
Жеђ је велика
И сада видим:
за оне с друге стране
тек неко лице овде
сија првобитном намером
неонских боја
Сва друга плешу
у самртном ропцу
непоклоњене пажње
Шушти болесна амбиција
и трзају лица
у кокитусу промашених снова
Веје снег

Amitabh Vikram Dwivedi

Burqa

Burqa
Since she refused to her daily suppression,
That burqa couldn't witness her assassination.
She only demanded little light and books.
No sinful act actually she undertook.
They singled her out as there was no forgiveness.
And soon they got back to their sinking business.
They used their guns and shot her in daylight.
But things only happen when God decides.
She passed her exam against that death;
And proudly became a voice of other oppressed.
Like a shining star for every wandering bark.
She became a light for women in the dark.
No veil can now hide her face divine.
Nor any burqa will ever shadow her shine.

Part IV

"IF I CAN'T DANCE TO IT, IT'S NOT MY REVOLUTION."
--EMMA GOLDMAN

Gerald Padilla

<u>I can't breathe</u>

Today I can't breath
No puedo respirar
As my brother is on the floor
With arms around his throat
Desperately gasping for his life

Today I can't breath
No puedo respirar
With his face pressed against the sidewalk,
six uniforms against one
A fallen brother
A fallen brother
Another one

Today I can't breath
No puedo respirar
I too inhale desperately
For I am my brother's keeper
And a wrong done to him
Is a wrong done to me.

Darrel Alejandro Holnes

Ferguson, USA

When life gives you strange fruit
how do you make lemonade?
When just to rent a business stand
you have to pay in spades?
Obesity is an epidemic,
too much sugar in the blood,
so do you instead just let the strange
fruit juice dry up?
Then eat its dried flesh like you do
sweet raisins in the sun?
Or do you let it hang there,
ripe and plump, for the crows to pluck?
Do you let its juices ferment into wine?
Swill it around in your glass and watch
its legs run down the side?
Do you bottle it up for sale?
Transport it in paper bags?
Use masking tape and blue pens
to make your own price tags?
And when that cop comes up to you,
do you offer him a cup?
Do you think that would be enough
for him to not charge you
with possession of illegal drugs?
When white boys are chugging
and keg-standing this shit?
When white girls are crying
to get another hit? And even
their parents are addicted to it.
You selling? The cop asks before,
uninvited, he takes a swig.
When he drinks he tastes ambrosia in the brew
and sees that he could pull the trigger
and make the same out of you.
What will you do then when the cop shoots
to drain your strange juice?
Will you let the bullet wound fester like a sore?

And when he keeps your blood on tap,
then will you not take it anymore?

In this Eden, where
a darker-the-berry state of mind
was our founding, is our fall,
will a sweet tooth lead to you
splattering a wall?
~ after Langston Hughes

Laura Cesarco Eglin

Listening

I'm trying to hold my breath
one word at a time. Silence is
too subtle to let it speak all
at once is slower when it comes
to discerning what is not heard.
Quiet is in the tongue
that subsides to language

The pace of water

She likes it when she
becomes an edge and spoils
the milk just by looking at it.
A drink of something else might
turn water white. After all
beets do wonders to transformation.
She likes it
when she sees connections. Her feet
on the ground and her hands
in the air is sometimes called
dancing and sometimes a calling
for help comes with lingering
jellyfish
the ones in those pictures can
just about make her
forget the pain of coming out
of the water, knowing the sea
made a statement, knowing how
to read the lines on her body,
knowing that people can live
in packs but not in schools

Miriam Damaris Maldonado

Mariposas Caribeñas

Escribo sobre mariposas
arrastrándose en garitas turísticas
transformándose en negras taínas
que lavan sus apellidos
en donde Pilato enjuagó sus culpas.

Todas ellas,
vírgenes prostitutas con los ojos enhebrados
de verdad, hermosas mojigatas,
aplastadas por el silencioso colectivo
asfixiadas con la colonial saliva.

Todas ellas, orugas en pleno vuelo
con la sangre pesada de bilí
marineras alojadas en Isla Nena
con el estiércol y el cáncer
forrados de prácticas militares.

Sobre mariposas
que deshojan herejes en hogueras
de un capitalino mármol
cuando su poesía yanqui vomita promesas.

Escribo sobre mariposas
que arden, muerden, arañan,
se vuelven magma
y renacen quebrantando un capullo de costillas.

Escribo sobre mariposas
que rescatan soñolientos coquíes
a viva voz, agachaditos,
a ritmo de bomba y plena
                              libertad.

Tom Murphy

Where did the EZLN fall?
Maybe respected life too much.
Could have gotten Las Casas to plead
Against Sepúlveda again   bitter pill.

Cock Brothers and Monsanto shame
Us to zip mouths with their chemical
Cash. We're all digitally hooked. No
Suckass end to the cops color war.

When you start believing the pigs
Are your friends that's worse than
Pacific Garbage patch! Corrupt FIFA,
no different than Tom Brady's
Saggy balls. My kids are going up and

They will inherit Gaia, deathbed edition.
Oh love, is not the problem, add a pint of respect.
Sancho and Isabella came together without
Regret. Expulsion! Gaza strip style. When the

Phoenicians came down the gangway, yelling,
Ya Basta better buy! Give 'em Strike. "It's free."

Kay Boyle Used to Live

Kay Boyle used to live
       up on Frederick
  round the corner years ago,
seen from the rosemary bush
and the portable low fire grill,
the neon cross-dubbed
       nuclear Jesus,
from the backyard a score or more later
on Clayton;
both those times _____ past.

     Ms. Boyle, these are words that somehow must be said.
Port Corpus Christi's gun and hummer running
   mixed with crude & MTBE additive has most peckerwood

rednecks standing proud.
   The Hispanic kids who've clawed their way free
from the backwater shanties for a piece of American
action abroad
pretend to be Hector Garcia
and his G.I. (Joe) forum
       clutch the promise that this land _____ good,
if you resist testing the soil, the water,
the air or the genetic make-up of the
crop circles.

Up in Iowa, Dragons protest
blood-for-cash ideal. Gatherings are
subpoenaed by the good ol' boy anti-terrorist
clan of   stockholder clowns.

During Louisville's outside smoke break,

          _____
the truncheon-line of clear gas masked horses.

     Unfettered of mind and duty,
exercise their rights
at the barricades _____ , bellowing stuck pigs.

Black tinted glass expeditions
with the red/blue flash
in the grill
_____overpower Main Street,
                    making for Gault House East's
          $2000 a blue-plate rubber _____ lunch
as
          the presidential motorcade sojourns like
midnight street race crackup
 near the barbacoa stand.

As I gaze out.
                    As I gaze out
          on this once fertile Land

                    To Tell Walt Whitman,
          This is not the ground Washington trod.
His resolve diminished after the
          horses drank the   diazinon flow;
          _____ to the earth.
                    1796 Farewell Address against foreign
Treaties & partnerships
                    might read more like Ike's 1961
Anti-Military Industrial Complex with overtones
towards the Ags.

Judge Scalia, how was that informative
          duck hunt in Louisiana with Barbital Cheney?
Did you turn your back when he excuses you from the blind?
          Were guaranties mentioned for those wavy justice stripes
that Rehnquist had Father McKenzie _____ in the night?

          Will you try to destroy women's rights for another century

or let this faction now in control roll
until terror's whipped from the world?
_____ the helicopters rove above the house.
          Simulations of HIV proved to come from _____
not what _____ was shredded before _____.

Are the cameras still on?

This George stares down the world
after buying from Wal-Mart's bearded lady
    all the duct tape and plastic

and awaits the toxic clouds to permeate the town's cerebellum
in his drag-queen-wig.

Paul Toth

<u>11 Bullet Catcher</u>

Reflecting upon a mask
that served a double task,
its steam-white dunes
an IOU of unsigned ruins,
deflected between
the aluminum screen
he whom he
loved above his other me
yet knew could not persist,
as though a remedy
said, "If the sun did not exist,
"it would be necessary
"to invent it."

       Neither wit
       nor reason,
       he spoke instead
       words ahead of season.

His wristwatch revealing
a deadline dimension,
he ended the suspension
of his concealing
and began the erasure
of the unsmiling
deserted, glacier
and saw the underlying
scape of moon,
craters deep, maroon,
scatter-shot stains
upon his scan,
youth's remains
of birth's misgiving,
and to himself he said
like the living
to the dead,
"I am not a man."

These words twice proved right,
for he became Afghanistan,
the sand of his inkling,
and whether day or night,
no more twinkling.

Alison Stone

Travesty

Skittles, iced tea, unarmed. Seventeen years
old. Looks like he's up to no good...he's just star-
ing at me. Though cops tell Zimmerman to stay
in his truck, he gets out to find a stre-
et sign.   Fox News anchors rave
about gold teeth, suspension, drugs. Show Trayv-
on pose tough, blow smoke. Never vary
the message. Mock Rachel Jeantel, her tart
tongue mumbling, That's real reta-
rded, sir. Dangerous. Dumb. Thug. The strate-
gy works. The dead kid's guilty. The defense can rest.

Mirror

I am white, I can feed silence.
My children can breathe, though
the air's fetid with fear
extinguished Black men
shared. Who will keen for
them? Outrage must be
boots on blood-stained streets. Can you hear
each victim's last words echo?

Each victim's last words echo.
Boots on blood-stained streets – can you hear
them? Outrage must be
shared. Who will keen for
extinguished Black men?
The air's fetid with fear
my children breathe. Though
I am white, can I feed silence?

PW Covington

Ranks and Files

I, too, once bought the lies of war
Medals and flags and bugles galore
I fell to place in ranks and files
And yearned to fly ten thousand miles

Then, there were those we flew back home
In boxes, dead, and all alone
But, dead, too, was something not yet known-
A chance to grow up, completely grown

Beyond parade route barricades
There breathes a world without berets
As rockets last red twilights' gleam
They return too, within my dreams

And a fuse once lit there, long ago
Has detonated in my soul
As I watch the TV and I see
The ranks and files replacing me

Searching for My Own Counterinsurgency

It's still out there
You know…
On The Road
If you have the eyes to find it
and if you listen with an ear for futility

It's in the turn lanes
Of the city streets
It's in doughnut shops in mid-afternoon
In bars right next to nail salons
In bail bond agents' waiting rooms
Laundromats always make me
Think of Ginsberg
and Alan Oak
That long walk to the highway
After they let you out of Del Valle Jail

It's the cats crowding the dumpster
Behind the Taco Bell
It's what churches and temples
Have always promised
It's a paperback library
Started by GI's somewhere
Surrounded by sandbags

It's that same, sad, sweater
You've worn for decades,
Bought at a thrift store
Someplace that it snowed

It's not trusting mirrors any longer
It's learning that lies
Have always been here
They are aboriginal in our DNA,
Twisted
Terrorists behind every freedom
Liberty and anonymity are the greatest dangers
You should never be unknown
The lie of omniscience

The lie of God
The lie of Love
The lie of good and evil and loss and luck
The lie of truth is out there, still
On The Road
If you've earned the eyes to look at it
And you were born with an ear for futility

Marcie Eanes

Walking Dead

Sitting on lap
a child is shot
Precious little girl
died at home
Buried with doll,
she's a cute angel
Free from worldly harm

Stting on lap,
a child is held
Adorable boy
raped and sodomized
at home
Secret shame, hidden pain
That crime waits
 to be told

While those in suburia
scorn inner cities,
Pristine hides
dark spirits too
The evil innocence hides,
kills all inside
Making them
walking dead
too

Youthful Indiscretion

Why did you change?
Did you forget the dinners
we shared, laughs we had
when we were young ?
I saw you
lingering outside after dates;
kissing my sister
when you gave her that promise ring
Those were no quick pecks
We made quite a team
the year we won state,
and those smooth dance moves
you showed on the dance floors,
put many to shame
You had it
goin' on!

Real life began
You stopped answering my calls
Chance meetings
turned into broken promises
time after time
if you acknowledged
my greeting
Imagine my hurt
the day cameras caught you
spouting racial untruths
without shame
My family watched, too,
remembering days
we welcomed you
into our home
back then...
You saw my father
exhausted from work,
come home
to his wife and kids
No liquor on breath
or roar in voice,

he invited you to stay
for supper

School reunions bring jokes
about youthful induscretions
Raucous laughter
about ghettos being sneaky playgrounds
Those who lived there
didn't zip off their skin
We opened our homes
in hospitality
I finally understand
what all that meant
Using people, playing games
in our neighborhoods
Anything to piss off
your bigoted father

Octavio Quintanilla

[Por la noche, los vecinos escarban fosas]

Por la noche, los vecinos escarban fosas.
Creen que no nos damos cuenta,
pero el ruido de los picos y las palas contra piedra
nos despiertan.
Creemos que son fosas para enterrarse,
o para enterrar a los hijos que les quedan.
La verdad, lo único que podemos hacer es imaginar.
De nuestros hijos, sabemos poco.
Ya no los leemos en los diarios.
Ya no los vemos en la televisión.
Ya no los escuchamos en los noticieros radiofónicos.
Algunos de nosotros todavía los buscamos
en las esquinas,
en los asientos traseros de los taxis,
en las banderas que anuncian patrias.
Allí no están.
Desaparecen las esquinas.
Desaparecen los asientos traseros de los taxis.
Desaparecen las banderas que no tienen patria
que anunciar.
Los vecinos nos despiertan con sus aullidos.
Auque sus lamparas abren la noche con su luz,
nunca les hemos visto los rostros.
Se nos ha olvidado el color de sus caras.
Cómo se llaman.
Cada mañana despertamos acariciando
una cajetilla de fósforos.
Nos sentamos en la esquina de la cama
y buscamos nuestro reflejo en el espejo.
Queremos asegurarnos que todavía estamos aquí,
mirar nuestros ojos y pensar
en la forma más fácil de quemar
lo que nos queda de vida.

[At night, our neighbors dig graves]

Translated by Sonya Groves

At night, our neighbors dig graves.
They think we don't see them,
but the noise from the picks and shovels against stone
wake us.

We think they dig graves to bury themselves,
or to bury the children that still live.
All we can do is imagine.
Of our children we know little.
We don't read about them in the papers.
We don't see them on television.
We don't hear them on the radio.
Some of us are still looking for them
on street corners,
in the backseats of taxis,
on the flags proclaiming countries.
They aren't there.
Street corners disappear.
The backseats of taxis disappear.
Flags that have no country to announce disappear.
The neighbors wake us with their howls.
Even though their lamps open the night with their light,
we've never seen their faces.
They have no skin color.
No names.
Every morning we wake
caressing a pack of matches.
We sit at the bed's edge
and look at our reflections in the mirror.
We want to be sure we're still here
so we can look into our eyes
and find the easiest way to burn
what's left of our life.

Balas

Hay balas que en su trayectoria
quieren convertirse en gotas de agua.
Otras se apresuran para extenderse en el blanco
como paraguas.
Hay balas disparadas para poner orden.
Otras escupidas para maldecir al mundo.
Esta bala fue fabricada para un animal,
esta otra para una mujer,
esta para un niño,
esta para un hombre blanco,
esta para un hombre negro.
La mordida de una bala desvanece
de el cuerpo, no
de la memoria.
Allí queda la marca de sus dientes.
La voluntad se dobla ante la amenaza
de una bala. Una bala
para hundirla en el cachete de un cerdo,
otra para dispararle al vagón de tren
que se cree vacío.
La bala no sabe quién se roba los cadaveres.
Cierra el hocico
en las interrogaciónes.
La engordeze el oficio de matar.
Ante la mirada agria de una bala,
el animal se traga el sollozo.
También el niño.
El hombre blanco.
El negro.
La mujer.
En el amor la bala chifla.
Acaba con el aburrimiento.
Preferible encontrar balas
que lenguaje.
Aprendemos a escribir con polvora.
Pastor de los sicarios, la bala.
Virgen para el rebaño
de ametralladoras.
Bendita la bala que te abre la boca
para que salgas por ella.
Esta vez, deja que sea Dios
el que jale el gatillo.

Bullets

Translated by Sonya Groves

In their path some bullets
want to transform themselves into raindrops.
Others rush to open like umbrellas
inside their target.

Some bullets are fired to keep order.
Others spit out to curse the world.
This bullet was made for an animal,
this other for a woman,
this one for a child,
this one for a white man,
this one for a black man.
A bullet's scar fades
on the body, not
in memory.
There, the bite remains.
The will doubles over before the threat
of a bullet. Bullet
for the swine's cheek.
Another to shoot a train car
believed empty.
A bullet doesn't know who takes the corpses.
It closes its snout
during questioning.
It fattens its skill to murder.

Before the sour look of a bullet,
an animal swallows its sob.
And so does a child,
a white man,
a black man,
a woman.
The bullet wolf-whistles at lovers.
It destroys boredom.
It's preferable to encounter bullets
than language.
We learn to write with gun powder.

Hitman's shepherd, the bullet.
Virgin for the flock
of machine guns.
Blessed is the bullet that opens your mouth
so that you may exit.
This time let it be God
who pulls the trigger.

Michael Aaron Casares

The Reality Age

There is nothing bombastic to say
removed from the very notion of reality.
There is only a dire need for truth and the
infinite illusion of said truth from anyone's
right to know.

The theories of human functions finding a method
to live and learn and experience. It is the experience
that has been taken away from man by whomever or
whatever entity shaped this plane of existence; they
have formed the arena we play in, controlling once natural
chances, and what could be.

They have distorted whole cultures, have downed entire
economies, have instigated genocide against several races.
They have caused starvation by blocking the passage of food
with necessary funding. They have caused death and disease
with deadly medicines and practices propagated by their greed.

They have confused the world into division, labeling every man
and nation, and magnifying their differences. They have stripped
us of our purity and turned spirituality into a quest of self-
righteousness.

They have turned our scholars into sadists, and our children into
apathetic slaves taught to climb the ladder. They have turned our
history over to purveyors of deceit whose ill-will seeks to poison the
many peoples of this earth.

They are the heads of corporations, the heads of state, the heads
military, media, and industry, the heads of education and academia.
From Google to Apple, from Yale to Harvard, from Goldman Sachs
to Viacom, from Monsanto to Pfizer and Merck, from Barclays
Bank to Microsoft; countless pharmaceuticals, countless military
contractors; life-term representatives that represent themselves; a
public wishing for peace or for everything to just go away, uncertain
to act or to remain on their knees.

This is the general mess
in this age of decision,
in this reality age of
imperfect vision,
unawake, unconnected,
the soul, the people
become discontented.

Steven Alvarez

yr migra blew up América

for maestro Baraka

0:11 down
0:12 well
0:13 the old debajo—
0:20 somebody love & of thinking
0:24t he hermanita is both domestically & internationally one . . .
0:29 used to cover the mierda of her masters—
0:32 dole . . . dome . . . dome . . . dome . . . drone . . . O . . . done . . .
0:36 the old somebody a—
0:40 they sey—is some . . . terrorist's liability & retina—
0:44 gets a head—it wuz in Maricopa County—claro
0:48 yes—uh that checks Latinos—how illegal are you you not me?
0:52 partner Sunday—tho it wuzn't sure a lot of . . .
0:56 or—presidente—do w/ virtually any partial
0:59 mexicharms—yells did the—
1:02 it wuzn't gonna be in the house to the White Sea diseases—that
were—
1:07 let people terrorized residents anything—
1:10 most humanity vomit as they please for
1:14 they sey they sd we want walls we want walls—
1:17 who do the same—who is this poll—
1:21 who's telling lies w/ the skies that no borders . . .
1:25 thoughts out the world's who got that plantations—that
privatized prison—
1:29 incarcecide in América—sideways levels
1:32 who all 28—
1:35 who cd show that's all narco bullet shells—
1:39 got this far—got sd this week—that matches & fires—
1:43 who kill sey they've got it—still little
1:47 cd be useful—who wuz the nameless brownface
1:51 who Jesús is available—who created every day
1:55 partner school grades—sey you only have a good look at it—
2:01 who define a lot of fun—science to me—bombs away—the guns
2:05 Google slaves—souls who call you—if they miss

189

2:10 who sey they always been seying all—
2:14 whose solo tengo—who sold me—
2:17 met this hemisphere every days or so we only northward gazed—
2:23 who all the buildings got the money—thank you—
2:26 money ... lots ... you up wallpapers all—
2:29 slave ship southward—well known army—little
2:32 nameless ones—who is the friend—who rules—
2:37 who were all older moms ... wuz a lot you got me
2:43 peace we think—the wall—more walls—
2:46 altho no toilets—& we want yr oil—let me do it—
2:53 who owns sales—who are on the air—along the walls
2:58 or rather the migra brown murderers—late last year—old—
3:02 will call you—who live in the biggest howls
3:06 who do the biggest line—who go on vacation anytime hun—
3:13 don't kill mostly—it's who kill all browns look a little—since
borders bind
3:17 ok—you're the most far-reaching—cables happen
3:21 & los Latinos
3:25 who all levels below the borders—
3:28 television or radio
3:32 even know me all hola Jose
3:36 & behold so they're also cities make the laws—
3:40 all who may wish to visit—who believe the confederate flag ...
3:44 ay baby—borderline concerned abt democracy ... & even I—
no!—in recent memory
3:51 sey you decide—didn't lose it ...
3:56 who did—everybody else got richer while the engine is ideal ...
4:01 previous to this wd change the bottle ...
4:05 wd you like most people—will do most people—who know what
abt survival
4:10 led the colonies solos to rule the world—
4:14 who sey only evil biggest sex education—a whole who all ...
4:20 who all ... who told you what you think—that you later like that
...
4:23 I'll bit—late—maybe sales—
4:27 okay—CIA who follows—altho
4:30 who always learn hot Mexical choices all the—
4:33 as a whole—who know—outside Arizona—visibility is low—
4:39 does it all ...

4:41 need fossil fuels—something going away—who make tutorials
4:45 get the biggest sales—hot weather—
4:48 conference against racism—who killed our neighbor—
4:53 who kill our neighbor—such a thing—are they going to the elderly
4:57 it will be it to make money painting velvet
5:02 polls close in Tijuana
5:05 al pastor tacos & carnitas of chins—same ones—& kill—
5:08 ruled out yeah
5:11 let me know—the one that's always—
5:15 laying they shd love Amurka—well that is all—
5:19 don't like Geronimo—
5:23 side put me on hold—already natural habitat of a sudden—who kill you—mean I
5:29 sd hey my case made . . .
5:32 also what theme wuz it once tribalism
5:39 press it who put in place . . .
5:42 closely it's a who wuz in Mexico . . . is it will
5:46 do it—who sent a letter also gave me a little soft sole
5:51 ajua!—wuz a lot simpler—lead metal into the rose is a rose
5:55 all the people are nice—torture assassinated managed—
5:59 the official abt you really—yeah—
6:02 satellite Califas Arizona New Mexico Texas sd
6:07 who got the most sensible—when the—
6:10 it's who the jurors in invisible cases—
6:15 go to jail if he hears—remain inside immigrant wars— all
6:21 who got shd roll back into power—who got but she's
6:24 that payload shithole—
6:29 who decided so that's it goals reconstruction the New Deal
6:34 year great societal—
6:37 who does our deporter-in-chief with 2,000,000 holes in his legacy—&
6:42 well . . .
6:43 cool the gusano—who know what got us—deported—
6:48 on the lease—the visa card—
6:54 calmly new w/ botas picudas
6:58 also scenario it polo—
7:02 pressure who wuz it wuz it he chatted with the boys in jail—
7:06 seying that when that narco met me let me know—when do I

start? —it is where all the

7:11 hollywood edits—

7:13 who sd that much—that all who need to chase it—wuz only a little

7:18 whose house is really white—as it went our stay—brown adobe home that day—

7:22 why did you all stay away—quotas rule—

7:26 explosion allow newspapers sey the devil's face to the CEO

7:33 to make money—whole—the who—might go

7:36 for sale who want the world like it's—

7:40 who wants a little like it—

7:43 national so hot that

7:47 bullets—who's most powerful—

7:51 well you know the seying—that but anybody seen the devil . . .

7:55 like analysis . . . believing in yr life

7:58 like an owl—tho the devil—altho I love—all day—

8:02 like that—all the schooling & fire—

8:05 we have questions—we'll play it like there wuz nothing crazy—

8:10 laugh our nalgas off a little while walls that whole us—

8:14 pin

8:21 do

8:41 do

demographics unit

now that you have completed the citizenship application you can
begin preparing for the naturalization interview—let's take a look
at what you can expect when you are invited to our hielo offices for
your citizenship interview . . . & open up yr retinas . . . one asunto
Mareea¬—two or three please—are you want to? Santa Mareea?
yes i am . . . demure . . . please raise your right hand—do you swear
to tell the truth—yes i do . . . please have a seat managed feeling
horrid impassable—what is your full name you failure—Pandemico
Paredes—where were you born? gurgle . . . do you wish a change in
name today? night tonight . . . wd you like your full name on your
certificate of citizenship? that wd be fine how did you come to this
country? allocation by my mother . . . & when did you become a
permit? I mean resident? . . . been a premier effort & fierce january
two thousand one—what is your birthday? born in june ni niteen
eighty four . . . how tall are you? five-feet exchanges . . . ok when was
the last time you traveled outside the united states? last dime travel
wantheeng tu thousan fi . . . & where did you go? . . . g . o . n . . . e .
. . did you stay outside the country for more than six months? jwas
gone for juan mon what other trips to take in the last five years? took
to my trips see wanted a comedian four days . . . I'm no—going—
no—to cheer for fi weeks . . . what is your address? eseventy-ford
feefty reegeline—infrequently—are you currently employed? yes i
wd add plumbing . . . are you married? Dead was yr wife a citizen?
not my wife was a permanent—how many times if you've been
married? only juan . . . do you have children? my daughter is juan
jear ol . . . & where did she live? Chile . . . sickening have you ever
claimed to be a citizen? have you ever registered to vote in the united
states? no ma'am do you pay your taxes? jes i do . . . have you ever
been in a mental institution? have you ever been a member of the
communist party? have you ever been a member of a terrorist group?
since becoming a permanent resident at you ever called yourself
a non-resident on any tax return? I'm sorry no . . . creative bigger
question—did you ever call yourself a non-resident on your tax
return? no i did not . . . have you ever committed a crime for which
you have not been arrested? have you ever been convicted of a crime
are on friends? have you ever going to jail? have you ever been a

prostitute? ever had any problems w/ alcohol or drugs? have you ever
helped anyone into the country illegally or lied to a government
official? have you ever been ordered removed excluded or deported
from the united states? have you ever served in the armed forces?
do you support the constitution & form of government of the united
states yet right now? do you understand the profiles of allegiance
to the united states? do you? yes I did . . . thought I did . . . what is
the oath of allegiance? it means that i am loyal to thees nayshon .
. . & buy many things . . . uh… water . . . alle fight for it . . . if the law
requires it . . . are you willing to bear arms on behalf of the united
states? slice my neck i wd . . . if the law requires that are you willing
to perform work of national importance under civilian direction? jes i
wd . . . okay sir are you ready to take the civics portion of the test? jes
jes right—how many states or their in the union? now if you speak
eight—what country did we fight during the revolutionary war?
we'd politicking statement—white is the constitution—if both the
president & vice president died who becomes president? the espeaker
of the casa—what are perfectly branches of government? one the
extricated two paired w/ paper & thirdly handed to the show—white
is congress—ice house of representatives—& if any—for how long
do we elect each senator? or—four years . . . that is incorrect it—six
years—but you don't have to answer them correctly—who is the
head of the executive branch of government? the president what by
the first ten amendments to the constitution called? that there are
facts—who sd—meet liberty or didn't do it—actually carry what is
the highest court in the united states? if the princely court—what
kind of government does the united states have? a republic—what's
special group takes precedent? the cabinet—okay that's good I'm
going to dictate two sentences to you here is a pencil . . . & paper . . .
please write the first sentence—are you ready? jyes i ham okay idu
light . . . living . . . Shelbyville . . . that is correct—here is the next
sentence—I don't want to be eight united states . . . that is correct—
congratulations! you let me ask your citizenship test—you will
become a citizen today please check there's paper—& make sure
that will be information is correct if you did—please initial yr name
where indicated—signed cover here—to my time in this line—please
write your entire name—& an initial here & also here—training you
learn—passport anger—newspaper—here too—indicate that you

passed your citizenship test—please complete this form also—by filling in your name—there—address—& checking no in all of these boxes—& then go back outside kindly in the waiting tank—they will pull your name in the next hour or so & when they do—please bring your green card . . . & therefore . . . to the window . . . & you have a—checking account—& you'll have to wait for the old—thank you very much—we have to—pay day ok—yes—congratulations—that when—warner—did not hear or understand the question—she asked the officer to repeat the question bc she did not—not bc she cd not understand it—

Kelly Talbot

Stoplight

White lines on the black street,
showing people where to drive,
showing people where to meet.
White man in a black car
sights a black man in a white shirt
and a black tie at the stoplight,
just a black guy with a white sheet full of black words
and a white guy full of white words like a white sheet
on a black street full of white lines
telling people where to drive,
telling people where to meet,
until the stoplight.

The black guy. The white guy. White shirts and black ties.
White words, black lines, black words, white lines,
on the black and white streets until the stoplight.
That's a red light on a black street full of white lines,
and the red light brings a black-and-white
with red-and-blue lights, blue shirts, black ties,
black sticks, and black guns at the red light,
and the black guy can't run, and he can't hide.
White men in their blue shirts with their black sticks.
Black man, but his white shirt's now a red shirt.

And the white man in his white shirt and his white tie
in his white car with his white sheets full of white words
follows white lines to the white streets of his white world
and his white lie.

Guilt

Teach me.
Soft cotton. I need to know how to be
soft, white cotton
so that when the weathered black fingers pluck me,
I will be ready.
Teach me.
I never had a spiritual,
and I don't want to send you back to Africa.
I am america,
and I am soft and white,
and I am fluffy, soft, and white
with bright red drops
from brown leather that bleeds
so that I may sleep on a soft, white cotton pillow.
I am a slave to being a master,
and nothing else matters,
and I don't want to be lazy,
but I can't cut my fingers,
and how you must hate me,
and how you must wish
that when your fingertips
pluck fresh white cotton
that the blood come from cotton
and not from flesh.

Celina A. Gómez

Appealing Citizenship
– Dallas, Texas—June 2008

Waiting single file, folders stacked
stamped welcome to America,
blue collar red economy filled
with white majority. Forget

your country and wave
this miniature flag dressed
church clothes found cheap
at the nearest ropa—flowers
printed pretty while mama y papa
grip each other

praying. Playing with the ribbon
in your hair, white—trying to look
american in a line full of people
who look just like you—lost

in a room of checking—rechecking
documents—reciting the national
anthem—in american

only. Finding your language
when you have done everything to lose it.
watching as the young Asian woman leaves

flagless, confused—sits crying off
to the side of the room, defeated—
sifting through red

rejection from a country that does not want

As Poet / As Teacher

I want

to write each
student into a poem where:
lines are defined by your
broken promises and their
potential that over—
whelms the poet. I want to write

each student as a poem
that spasms and twists and breaks
out into their greatness. into Alé
who as a faded heart-shaped birth
mark on the right side of her nose
that extends into the differences
between her and her twin
sister who sits directly behind

her during testing. They reach
for a dictionary in the same way—hopeful
but heavy. Alé works slowly, slower
each page turn meticulous, exacting her success
while her sister sits behind, always

like Arron who writes into
broken sentences: I cannot
finish. He turns in his test
only partially complete because
he cannot write. Five lines out
of twenty six spelled out his failure.

They are not my students but that
is only a way to shift the blame
like the system—keeps on shuffling

failure onto the faces of potential
of futures
of Robert
of Luis

of Maggie
of Maria
of Angel
of Manny
of Sandy who went to school each day with fear of her parents'
deportation.
of Alex who was brilliant but dropped out because his brilliance was
wrong for the system.
of Edgar who was sent to AEP four times for possession and was
forced to graduate early.
of Samantha who dates Edgar and is labeled just the same.
of Juan who was in Loco 13 and dropped out.
of Albert who was called "El Flaco" but left that only to be denied
entrance to college.

Each student is a poem
innumerable and beautiful
and painful but

true. Do not force me
to lie. Teach truth
and power and possibility.
I write my students into
poems into my life into
a power that cannot be
enough. It is not
enough. Grow, poet,
teacher, so they can
have hope.

Ken Jones

THE LIE

The Lie grew as it spread.
The Lie, told often enough,
gathered inertia to its false core.
The Lie boldly intwined itself like DNA
into every being it encountered.
The Lie is that this material plane has any meaning.
The Lie is that we control our own destiny,
are not experimental animals
Aliens look upon as fodder or food.
The Lie soon consumed my entire hard drive.
The Lie was a massive space hog.
The Lie held my silent anger
The Lie kept my soul from grace.
The Lie bought me a few more days of ingratitude,
The Lie, mixed with a dollop of indifference,
Served me well in any social situation.
The Lie became my life which became my unknown truth.
The Lie was a path to the Great Spirit
I spent my waking hours cursing and embracing,
The Lie became the last friend I could trust.

IMAGINE PEACE

I. FORGOTTEN

In your frenzied palsy of prophecy
You will be forgotten
Like the long dead pickled in photographs
Or boys' toys in silent celluloid
You will be forgotten
From Iceland to Maui
The black volcanic rock survives
You will be forgotten
From Belize to Chile
Praise goes to pirates and Pinochets
But you will be forgotten
As you scramble to scribble
A few desperate phrases before they evaporate
You will be forgotten.

II. DECLINE

Poets confront the void
They yearned to fill
Now burn to avoid,
With the thirst of the sickly dehydrated
Their temporal lobe satiated
Begging for the taste of wet ecstasy
When the Muse soaked all cells
With life affirming spells
From a potion pouch theirs to command

Bumping the empty cloth bottom
In panic, they spew "Muse! Where are you?"
Long used to smooth Magic
Poets know through heightened eyes
When the void wins.

Jessica Helen Lopez

Diana the Huntress
[originally published in cunt.bomb.]

They say the number four bus enjoyed a certain reputation
its tires swaggering down a hilly road pockmarked by sage brush
loose in the axle like a man with too many beers under his belt

the fear exhaled from the women's nostrils
fueled the trek – a hot mist moist with the tang of terror
bus windows fogged by morning vapor
opaque and rheumy long after the women had vacated their seats

I took a pistol and placed a bullet into the bus driver's temple
easily I deposited it there
the sun made a wistful track along the soot-covered sky
and the maquilas shut their metal doors against the day
El Paso glittered like a City of Gold from the other side of the border
a muffled silence settled into all of our bones

at the arrival of the next dawn
I took a second bullet
silver as a single bead from the rosary my mother wore around her
neck
pregnant in the womb of the chamber
the bullet spat with quickfire and lodged
into the second man's brain

again no pity, no sorrow-colored remorse
only the old number four tossed like a tin can
I walked away and did not run from the
dead man bloated and gray faced
is back and arms laced with the scarred
scratches made by the women who had not got away

The newspapers jabbered like angry bees
and the AP wire was alive with the electricity of my name

Diana the Huntress
and I fear no moon, Lady of Wild Creatures

203

La Cazadora worshipped by the womanly workforce
of Juarez

My sisters are frightened mares

Some might say I will perish in hell with the rest of them
the men – adept at removing women's faces
removing their breasts like too-soon petals
the milk of their skin, the floating flotsam
peeled beneath the killer's knife

They like to leave behind bite marks on the buttocks
They like to leave behind dead babies cradled within eviscerated
wombs

Decomposed flesh resting inside decomposed flesh

And should I burn in the seventh layer
it is of no consequence to me
place me in hell and I will kill them all again

should my skin peel from my bones
incinerated by the heat of the oldest sin
I will always think it worth it
judge me Creator for I fear no moon

no man
no law
no lawlessness
no rampage

We are not our father's daughters
Our husband's wives
We are our mother's weeping

I only ever wanted to fashion birds with these hands
I only ever wanted soft righteousness not a countryside
riddled with the husks of dead raped women

They were like wild mustangs, the dark-eyed girls, cuckolded
shepherded to the slaughter; knees like young colts,

necks bared and naked breasts an offering to the swine

All of their holes raped, looted and left to spoil
the assembly plants are swollen with the limbs of women
the dirt is caked with their blood

Don't you know
It was you
who wrought me?

Wrenched me from my terrible anger
dug out from the shell of my sleep with a dirty fingernail
my rebirth whispered
upon the dying lips of women
one last jewel of blood dropped to the floor

reaping
sowing

beseeching
vengeance

one fine golden
and glorious
day

The Bodysmooth Consumer is a First World Woman

For we are all factory with smooth metal legs and consumable parts
Necks like smokestacks and Bic blades pink on a frosty Sunday
morning
We are sexy consumers and passive violent offenders, sleek credit
card swipe and mad jangle of the gold coin rising. We are third world
racketeers. The bodysmooth consumer of a first world woman.
We are debt and glory. We are wrinkle free foreheads and frozen
crow's feet.
We have no time for time.
For we are hot breath hangover and hot yoga class two for one
so we take our best hung over friend and sip Bloody Mary's post-bliss
For we are all about dancing on barstools and kissing cigarettes into
ring shaped smoke. We are ass shake and bend-over-hos. We are
bendable.
For we wear ladders for shoes and tower over our competitors.
We are stealth and young forever.
Venerate the artificial breast and its swooning sloshing beauty. The
rhinoplasty and the third
first world nose job. Admire the toe worship. The bejeweled cuticle.
The summer diet. The winter diet.
The spinach puree cleanse. Admire the summer house in the
Hamptons. The ski season in the Aspens.
The Mexican maid. The Korean maid. The Honduran maid. The
Venezuelan maid.
The breast milk by proxy.
Praise the glitter song. The tiara. The sexy five-year olds on parade.
The barroom brawl lyrics and the maddening microwaves and UV
lighting. Keep clipping coupons girl. You are almost there.
You are 957 Ways to Turn Him On. You are 101 Recipes for a Skinny
Bitch. You are the latest anti-aging technology. You are obsession. You
are infatuation. You are beautiful neurosis.
For we are Summer's Eve mask-the-smell make-overs. The polite
douche bottle beneath the bathroom sink. The tucked-away tampons.
We are hairless bodies - waxed, tucked, plucked, fucked, goosed, and
chemical peel. We are overcrowded mouth and bleached cusped.
This, for all the women whose hearts hum electric.
Whose hearts are shrink wrapped cadavers.
Whose hearts have been deodorized.
We who palpitate with key strokes and Facebook posts. We who stir

with caffeinated online purchases. We who gulp pharmaceuticals and
green-eyed margaritas. We who haunt drug stores and strip malls.
Go
to sleep.

Sleep. Sleep soft.

Sleep hard. All the signs are mounting.
They point to sleep. The mellifluous halo of stillness.
The small explosions behind the eyelids like white static
chrysanthemums.
Your middle name isn't happy hour. It isn't Eau de Parfum. You are
not your nervous breakdown.
You are 200,000 years of slanted rain. You are Lilith rising, bald and
golden-headed baby. You are Thought Woman and a satchel of eggs
webbed to your eighth leg. You are the squall and thunderous storm.
Your femur, the longest mile. Your body, anything but smooth, and
never a factory.
Never a cog or mechanic fulcrum. Never a this for a that.
We are rough-patch hewn of the fossil. The calcified woman.
We were here first.

Rossy Evelin Lima

43 Hechos ausencia

Mis 43 hermanos se hicieron ausencia
pero su lucha es de carne.

Me duele no haberles puesto cascabeles
para poder encontrarlos
en una de tantas fosas sin nombre,
me duele no haberles dado
la antorcha con la que crucé a este país
para tener una nueva vida,
me duele ver sus rostros en una lista
encabezada por la palabra masacre.

Sí, me duele, pero encarnecida tengo la vergüenza.

No supe ver que se los llevarían,
sus pancartas fueron cotidianas,
las muertes que avisaban su destino
fueron números perdidos
entre las urgencias de mi vida.

Me duelen sus huesos,
su sangre, hecha humo
inhalada por animales
armados y ciegos,
me duelen los kilómetros
que no recorrí con ellos,

Pero atragantada tengo la vergüenza.

Mis 43 hermanos están hechos ausencia
y yo no pude hacer nada.

Fue el gobierno, que manda
gracias a mi indiferencia
fue el gobierno
que no escucha

nuestras voces fragmentadas
fue el gobierno,
y yo no pude hacer nada.

Mis 43 hermanos
hoy vienen a despertarme
me han dicho con su ausencia
que de mis ojos debe caer el velo
para dejar de ver solamente mi causa,
que sacuda de mi cuerpo el estupor.

Me dijeron que sobre las luchas de raza, poder,
territorio y género,
se encuentra la responsabilidad
con nuestros hermanos,
me dijeron que arroje de mis manos
el cinismo que fermenta la buena vida,
porque salir a buscar el cambio
            será la única manera de hallarlos.

Así será nuestro encuentro.
43 ausencias
se convertirán en 43 millones de hermanos
resucitando en el asfalto
nuestro futuro.

A mis 43 hermanos los hicieron ausencia
pero aquí nos dejaron su huella, su lucha,
la rabia y el cambio.
La victoria será nuestro encuentro.
Todos somos Ayotzinapa.

Christopher Carmona

A Letter for Waiting

I am waiting for Lawrence Ferlinghetti...to tell me what to write
next...I am waiting for nothingness... for something to happen...
but nothing ever happens here...I am waiting for the sparrow to turn
red...and whisper that justice in Ferguson is real...I am waiting for
the tooth fairy to take my teeth and leave money under my pillow ...
but the tooth fairy doesn't want one tooth...it wants them all...I am
waiting for 43 students to return from Guerrero...I am waiting for
#Ayotzinapa to mean more than digital cries in a tumblr-verse...I
am waiting for brown rabbits to turn white so they won't be asked for
papers at checkpoint...I am waiting for tattooed bruises to disappear
from women's faces...I am waiting for the tree of liberty to be
refreshed by blood of patriots...not its tired huddled masses...

I am waiting for scissors to cut more than paper...I am waiting for
paper to be stronger than printed lies...I am waiting to tell myself
that less rocks and more talk will change the world...I am waiting
for another gunman and his student-riddled bullet ride...so we can
talk about change...because we live in nothingness...where only
talk is allowed...action is terroristic/ treasonous/ and serves only
the 99%...I am waiting for bones to unbreak...for guns to unshoot...
for death to give birth to life...and not the other way around...I
am waiting for snails to run faster than cheetahs...I am waiting for
songs to cure AIDS and paintings to rid us of poverty...not give us
money...but enrich lives so that dollars don't dance in heads like
sugarplums on Christmas...I am waiting to give America a pack of
crayons with all the colors of the world because she only has white
& black. I am waiting for people to see more black and white movies
so they can finally appreciate the wonders of purple lilacs and yellow
sunflowers...

I am waiting for poetry to be written on walls and art to be written
down in books...I am waiting for a tomorrow that will start night
and end day...I am waiting for white sheets with eyeholes to once
again by visible to the world...I am waiting for the avante garde
to list its assets on Craigslist...in the personals...LFSJ (looking for
social justice) without LHB (light human bondage)...I am waiting for
barrios to echo in the halls of Casa Blanca...I am waiting for

brothers not to be shot down like paper targets in a shooting range...
I am waiting for you, choke hold that killed Eric Garner, to apologize.
I am waiting for someone to actually hear I can't breathe and do
something about it. I am waiting for the 6 bullets buried deep in
Michael Brown to admit they knew they shouldn't have been there.
Did you see hands in air, bullets? Black man on knees? Or did you
only see the demon named blackness in the mind of whiteness made
to feel like little babies with guns? What about you gun that thought
you were a Taser? Leaving poor Oscar Grant on a stop he will never
exit. What about you hoodie? Were too menacing to walk down a
white street in Florida armed with skittles and iced tea, and Trayvon?
I am waiting for an answer.

I am waiting for Anonymous to hack through the lies of racism and
dump its emails on the internet...showing us that it only eats greed...
drinks contempt and watches ignorance on Youtube like porn...I am
waiting...I am waiting...I am waiting for brown kids with Spanish
skin and whitewashed minds to paint their lives purple like that cow
Socrates...I am waiting for poets to have a retirement plan that pays
off before they are dead...I am waiting for Mark Strand to come back
from the dead...like some zombie poet with only a hunger for flesh
ideas...I am waiting for Robin Williams to unkill himself...and teach
us about the importance of sucking the marrow out of life...I am
waiting for Bill Cosby to unrape all those women...and just be funny
again...I am waiting for Howl to be taught in kindergarten...I am
waiting for the streets to keep burning so we can always see white
cops in the dark...I am waiting for this poem to change the world...I
am waiting for the impossible...and I know it...

#54Ayotzinapa

[Found poem inspired by a poem by Lupe Mendez]

1. Abel García Hernández
2. Abelardo Vázquez Periten
3. Adán Abrajan de la Cruz
4. Manuel Angel Diaz
5. Alexander Mora Venancio
6. Antonio Santana Maestro
7. Benjamín Ascencio Bautista
8. Carlos Iván Ramírez Villarreal
9. Trayvon Martin
10. Carlos Lorenzo Hernández Muñoz
11. César Manuel González Hernández
12. Christian Alfonso Rodríguez Telumbre
13. Michael Brown
14. Christian Tomás Colón Garnica
15. Cutberto Ortiz Ramos
16. Dorian González Parral
17. Emiliano Alen Gaspar de la Cruz
18. Everardo Rodríguez Bello
19. Felipe Arnulfo Rosas
20. Oscar Grant
21. Giovanni Galindes Guerrero
22. Ricardo Diaz Zeferino
23. Israel Caballero Sánchez
24. Israel Jacinto Lugardo
25. Jesús Jovany Rodríguez
26. Tlatempa Jonás Trujillo González
27. Tamir Rice
28. Jorge Álvarez Nava
29. Jorge Aníbal Cruz Mendoza
30. Jorge Antonio Tizapa Legideño
31. Jorge Luis González Parral
32. Sandra Bland
33. José Ángel Campos Cantor
34. José Ángel Navarrete González
35. José Eduardo Bartolo Tlatempa
36. José Luis Luna Torres
37. Joshvani Guerrero de la Cruz
38. Julio César López Patolzin
39. Joel Acevedo
40. Julio César Ramírez Nava

41. Leonel Castro Abarca
42. Luis Ángel Abarca Carrillo
43. Freddy Gray
44. Luis Ángel Francisco Arzola
45. Magdaleno Rubén Lauro Villegas
46. Marcial Pablo Baranda
47. Marco Antonio Gómez Molina
48. Martín Getsemany Sánchez García
49. Mauricio Ortega Valerio
50. Eric Garner
51. Miguel Ángel Hernández Martínez
52. Miguel Ángel Mendoza
53. Zacarías Saúl Bruno García
54. Jessie Hernandez

Corina Carmona

<u>Grotesque Heads</u>

Contributor's Bios:

<u>Chuck Taylor</u> continues to be outraged daily but protects himself from losing it by heavy doses of humor. He has written in protest of heavy incarceration (Poet in Jail), laboratory use of animals (Song of Rising Consciousness), environmental destruction (When the Land is Taken), and the situation of the homeless, the poorly paid, and men's rights (Drifter's Story). He is rather solitary, mild mannered, shy, and quiet, but has been in protests at the Texas state capital, at a nuclear bomb manufacturing site near Amarillo, and against clear cutting in the east Texas piney woods, where he was jailed for chaining himself to a tree.

<u>Eduardo Quintero</u> (art) is a Contemporary mixed media painter who was born and raised in McAllen, Texas. He received his Bachelors of Fine Arts degree in studio art from the University of Texas-Pan American in 2005, followed in 2011 by his Master of Fine Arts degree with two-dimensional specialization from the University of Texas-Pan American. At the same time that he was completing his MFA, he also earned a Graduate Certificate in Mexican American Studies. He is currently an Adjunct Professor at both South Texas College and at the University of Texas Rio Grande Valley.

<u>Isaac Chavarria</u> is a pocho with an MFA in Creative Writing from the University of Texas-Pan American. He assists non-profit organizations in producing chapbooks for workshop participants. His poems are in The Acentos Review and Rio Grande Review online. His first book of poetry called Poxo won the NACCS Tejas Foco Best Poetry Book of 2013. Ultimately, he hopes the term pocho will represent a positive identity rather than a pejorative. He is the Executive Director of The Coalition of New Chican@ Artists.

<u>Vimeesh Maniyur</u> is an established bi-lingual poet, novelist and translator from kerala, in India. He has two volumes of poetry and a children's novel in his credit. He has also penned stories and dramas. He has bagged for many prestigious awards such as Culcutta Malayali Samajam Endownment, Madras Kerala Samajam, Muttathu Varkki Katha Puraskaram etc. for young writers in kerala.

<u>Me'ira Pitkapaasi</u> is a professor at a major university and two small urban community colleges. She is an experienced teacher of over thirty years, and she has been a foster parent for two and a half

decades. Ms. Pitkapaasi has been a writer for more years than she can count. She works primarily in multi-ethnic below-poverty environments, and fosters primarily disabled children.

Ogunsina Temi-tope (a.k.a Topid da poet) is a performing poet, journalist, from Oyo State, Nigeria. His performances and poetry address many societal issues and have been well received both locally and internationally. He started Writing since age nine. During his secondary school days, he wrote a soundtrack for the drama Dreams Comes True. His poetry has been featured in a number of anthologies: I Am Poetry (2013), Fearless poets against Bullying (2014), Emanation: foray into forever (2014),and lnk spot written collection (2014), poetry society of india anthology (2015), and 'Reclaiming our voices anthology(2015).

Lynn White lives in north Wales. Her work is influenced by issues of social justice and events, places and people she has known or imagined. She is especially interested in exploring the boundaries of dream, fantasy and reality. Her poem 'A Rose For Gaza' was shortlisted for the Theatre Cloud 'War Poetry for Today' competition in October 2014 and has since been published in the 'Poetry For Change Anthology by Vending Machine Press.

Raúl Sánchez is a translator currently working on the Spanish version of his inaugural collection "All Our Brown-Skinned Angels" nominated for the 2013 Washington State Book Award in Poetry. A 2014 Jack Straw Writers member. Also one of the mentors and judges for the 2014 Poetry on Buses project sponsored by 4 Culture and King County Metro. Last October, he participated in the TEDx Salon event in Yakima, WA titled: "How Creativity Heals" available on YouTube.

Susan Beall Summers has been writing poetry from a young age. Her first collection of poetry, Friends, Sins & Possibilities was published in 2011. She is an active Austin poet, member of Austin Poets International, Austin Poetry Society, and Writer's League of Texas. Her poems appear in Ilya's Honey, Texas Poetry Calendar, Lifting the Sky: Southwestern Haiku and Haiga, Harbinger Asylum, Small Canyons Anthology, Di-Verse-City, and others.

Kushal Poddar was born in a warm corner of India, a lone child and brought up with his shadow mates. He began writing verses at the age of six. He adopted his second tongue as the language to dream on. Widely published in several countries, prestigious anthologies included Men In The Company of Women, Penn International MK etc. and featured in various radio programs in Canada and USA and collaborated with photographers for an exhibition at Venice and with performers for several audio publications. He is presently living at Kolkata and writing poetry, fictions and scripts for short films when not engaged in his day job as a counsel/ lawyer in the High Court at Calcutta. He authored, The Circus Came To My Island and his forthcoming books are Kafka Dreamed Of Paprika and A Place For Your Ghost Animals.

Mariah Stettner is a poet and artist by night and a West Texas field engineer by day. Her work is typically of a socio political nature so this anthology is right in tune with her motivations to write. She has been published in several anthologies including the one produced for Waco WordFest, Permian Basin beyond 2014, as well as High Grade, Colorado School of Mines' literary arts journal.

M. Miranda Maloney is the founder of Mouthfeel Press, and the author of The Lost Letters of Mileva (Pandora Lobo Press 2014). Her work has appeared in or is forthcoming in the Bellevue Literary Review, MiPOesias, The Más Tequila Review, Texas Weather: An Anthology, Acentos Review, Huizache, and other national and international journals. She is the Educational Outreach Coordinator for the Smithsonian Latino Virtual Museum, and editor for the BorderSenses Literary & Arts Journal.

Farwa Naqvi is an MFA candidate at the University of Texas RGV where she also conducts Comp Con knoCkV as a TA. She's usually a very polite person, but certain topics - such as social injustice and human rights - impassion her to speak out, often through writing. She presented her nonfiction piece, "A Modest Woman," at the 2014 Festival of International Books and Arts and her work has appeared in the Monitor, including "Chasing Ghosts," a travel article on London.

Jasminne Mendez is an award winning author, performance poet and educator. Mendez has performed her poetry in venues all around Houston, including the MFAH, Rice and the Alley Theatre. She has shared the stage with respected writers and poets, notably, Sandra Cisneros and Taylor Mali. Mendez has been published both nationally and internationally and her first multi-genre memoir Island of Dreams was published by Floricanto Press in November of 2013.

Manuel Martinez is the author of four novels: Crossing, (Bilingual Press, 1998), Drift, (Picador USA, 2003), Day of the Dead, (Floricanto Press, 2010) and Los Duros (Floricanto Press, 2014). His fiction deals primarily with the lives of Mexican Americans and Mexican immigrants, and explores the themes of migration, contemporary urban life, and the experience of dislocation. He is also the author of a book of literary criticism, Countering the Counterculture: Rereading Postwar American Dissent from Jack Kerouac to Tomas Rivera, (University of Wisconsin Press, 2003).

Gerard Robledo is a Latino poet from San Antonio, Texas. He is currently a candidate in the online MFA program at the University of Texas at El Paso and holds a B.A. in English Literature with a focus in Creative Writing from Texas State University. Robledo's poetry and Spanish language poetry translations & critical works have appeared in Voices de la Luna: A Quarterly Poetry and Arts Magazine, Texas Poetry Calendar, and The Thing Itself.

Carolyn Adams' poetry and art have appeared in journals and anthologies such as Caveat Lector, Common Ground Review, and Voices in Wartime, among others. She has edited literary journals, and is the author of four chapbooks, the most recent being The Things You've Left Behind. She has been nominated for a Pushcart Prize, and was a finalist for the post of 2013 Houston Poet Laureate.

David Sapp is a writer, artist and professor living along the southern shore of Lake Erie in North America. His poems have appeared widely in a number of venues across the United States, in Canada and the United Kingdom. His publications also include articles in the Journal of Creative Behavior; chapbooks Close to Home and Two Buddha; and his novel, Flying Over Erie.

SPIRIT THOM is an improvising bard who plays best with improvised (live)music. He has hosted EXPRESSIONS First Saturdays for 17 years, and now hosts RAD RADAM READINGS Wednesdays in South Austin. He has 200 books of poetry available via worldpoetry. org, a derelict website and blog, eBooks, iTunes and is best enjoyed LIVE or on YOUTUBE. Thom believes his BEST poem is his NEXT poem!

Gabriel H. Sánchez is a writer and poet from South Texas. He has been published in scientific journals, in scholarly publications, several anthologies, and has served as a transcriptionist/ translator for a Rio Grande Valley newspaper. His first book of poetry is called The Fluid Chicano. He is a graduate of the University of Texas Pan American with a Master of Science in Rehabilitation Counseling. Alongside writing, Gabriel is also an actor, having played the role of President Lyndon Baines Johnson in the play titled Pat and Lyndon by Archer Crosely. He writes a blog titled "Cross Sections" on his company website, www.thervaingpress.com. Gabriel is also a freelance writer with his most recent articles published through Yahoo! Voices as a Yahoo! Contributor Network member.

Sarah Rafael García is a writer, community educator and traveler. Since publishing Las Niñas in 2008, she founded Barrio Writers and obtained a M.F.A. in Creative Writing. Her writing has appeared in Connotation Press, LATINO Magazine, Contrapuntos III, among others. Most recently, she was granted an Artist-in-Residence for her work titled Santana's Fairy Tales. Sarah Rafael is the editor for the Barrio Writers annual anthology and co-editor for the forthcoming Pariahs anthology.

Michael Verderber is a Texas playwright who specializes in writing plays and disjointed poetry. He has two books - "[nonspace]: theatre off the stage" and "Twas the FLOP Before Xmas" and has been published by VAO Press, and tNY Press. He is the recent winner of Playwright's Express's "Best Comedy" for his play "GPS" (tie for first) in LA.

Dustin Pickering is owner of Transcendent Zero Press, a Houston-based poetry publisher. He recently attended Matwaala, a South Asian Diaspora event, to celebrate the release of a collection of poetry and prose the press released. He is published in di-verse-city 2013 and 2015, Texas Poetry Calendar 2016, Seltzer, Lost Coast Review, Dead Snakes, Vagabonds, and many other journals. He was interviewed for Poetry is Dead, a documentary arranged by Weasel Press. He is author of the collection The Daunting Ephemeral. He was a feature at Houston's most popular reading series Public Poetry in 2013, and was Special Guest Poet for Austin International Poetry Festival that same year.

Pilar Rodríguez Aranda is a translator, an award-winning video artist, and a poet. Her poems have been included in dozens of magazines and anthologies in the American and European continents, and translated into English, Arabic, Greek, Italian and German. She is also an ARTivist, coordinator of 100 Thousand Poets for Change, Mexico, and a member of the Writing for Peace Advisory Panel.

Francisco X. Alarcón, award-winning Chicano poet and educator, is the author of thirteen books of poems that include six acclaimed bilingual poetry books for children. His most recent books are Borderless Butterflies / Mariposas sin fronteras (Poetic Matrix Press 2014) and Canto hondo / Deep Song (University of Arizona Press 2015). He is the founder of the Facebook page "Poets Responding to SB 1070." He teaches at the University of California, Davis.

Baljeet Singh has just finished Hindi Journalism from University of Delhi, Delhi. He's been into freelance writing and editing. He became Editor of Campus Sandhan, a newspaper produced by Hindi Department, University of Delhi. He has various publications in national and international journals. He was awarded by Hindi Academy, Delhi and published in Sahitya Akademi's journal. He loves photography. In future, he would like to research on Sex Crimes and Psyche of Criminals.

Juan Carlos Castrillón is the author of five books of poetry: Datura, Periferia, Cuaderno de Poerta en Sexto año, Cantos del Pueto, publicados por la editorial etreno Femeníno) Blues De Amor y odio, Canción Ineludible al Hombre que vendrá. Mejor Arder que Irse Desvaneciendo (Cuentos) . He is also author of Árbol en Llamas (Antologuie contemporary poets) and La Subversión Poética del Rock(translations and essays) both in Sediento Ediciones. Also recorded the album Clandestinos y Nocturnos with his musical project of poetry-blues La Decena Trágica.

Abigail Carl-Klassen's work has appeared in Cimarron Review, Guernica: A Magazine of Art and Politics, Post Road and Huizache, among others, is anthologized in New Border Voices (Texas A&M University Press) and won the Manitoba Magazine Publishers Association Award for Best Suite of Poems in 2014.

Anna Betts is Midwest born and raised poet, wife, and mother. She recently retired from the customer service field to focus on writing full time, for right now mostly she is a struggling artist. She's been published in a few on line publications, Red Fez, Bay Laurel and a few others. She is also a regular contributor on sites such as The Pen Central Wikinut and All Poetry.

henry 7. reneau, jr. writes words in fire to wake the world ablaze: free verse illuminated by courage that empathizes with all the awful moments, launching a freight train warning that blazes from the heart, like a chambered bullet exploding inadvertently. His poetry collection, freedomland blues (Transcendent Zero Press, 2014), was released in September of 2014. He also has an e-chapbook, entitled physiography of the fittest (Kind of a Hurricane Press), which was released in December of 2014.

Sarah Frances Moran is a writer, editor, animal lover, videogamer, queer Latina. She thinks Chihuahuas should rule the world and prefers their company to people 90% of the time. Her work has most recently been published or is upcoming in The No Se Habla Espanol Anthology, Drunk Monkeys, Rust+Moth, Maudlin House and The Bitchin' Kitsch. She is Editor/Founder of Yellow Chair Review.

Ofelia Faz-Garza is a mama, writer, and community advocate from North Texas who sounds proper on paper but enjoys a good mitote. She is a member of the DFW Latino Writers and North Tejas Writers groups, and a Community Voice for the Dallas Morning News. Her work captures the subtleties of life and celebrates the daily rituals that keep us rooted.

David Hale is a native of San Antonio, Texas and a recent graduate of Our Lady of the Lake University where he taught freshman composition. Currently, David is pursuing his MFA in Creative Writing at the School of the Art Institute of Chicago. David's writing is the product of the lessons he has learned in thirty years of life. Previously, David was published in both the 2014 and 2015 Texas Poetry Calendar.

Amitabh Vikram Dwivedi is university faculty and assistant professor of linguistics at Shri Mata Vaishno Devi University, India; and author of three books-two on lesser known Indian languages: A Grammar of Hadoti (2012) and A Grammar of Bhadarwahi (2013); and one poetry collection in Hindi titled: "Chinar ka Sukha Patta" (Dried leaves of Chinar), (2015). As a poet, he has published more than hundred poems in different anthologies, journals, and magazines worldwide.

Until recently, his poem "Mother" has been included as a prologue to Motherhood and War: International Perspectives (Eds.), Palgrave Macmillan Press (2014).

Darrel Alejandro Holnes' poems have been previously published in Best American Experimental Writing 2014, Poetry Magazine, Callaloo, and elsewhere in print and online. I am the co-author of PRIME: Poems and Conversations (Sibling Rivalry Press, 2014) and co-editor of the forthcoming Happiness, The Delight-Tree: An Anthology of Contemporary International Poetry in honour of the United Nations International Day of Happiness. He teaches creative writing at NYU and Rutgers University.

Erika Said's book iPoems: poetry in shuffle was published in Mexico in 2013 and will be launched in its bilingual version in 2015 by Slough Press. Her work was awarded first place in the 2012 Bi-national Contest "Letras en el Estuario" and in the 2014 Creative Writing UTSA Graduate Award. She has also received honorary mention in the short story state contest "Rosa de Castaño" and in the literary contest for Along the River II. Her work appears in six regional and national anthologies such as "Stories from the basement" (Mexico City, 2012), "Woman's Scream: Rebel Poetry" (Mexico City, 2011) and "Hell is a Caress" (Mexico City, 2011).

Laura Cesarco Eglin is the author of three collections of poetry, Llamar al agua por su nombre (Mouthfeel Press, 2010), Sastrería (Yaugurú, 2011), and Los brazos del saguaro (Yaugurú, 2015). A selection of poems from Sastería was translated collaboratively into English with Teresa Williams, and subsequently published as the chapbook Tailor Shop: Threads (Finishing Line Press, 2013), Cesarco Eglin's poems and translations have appeared or are forthcoming in a variety of journals, including Modern Poetry in Translation, MiPOesias, Eleven Eleven, Spillway, Puerto del Sol, Copper Nickel, Tupelo Quarterly, Columbia Poetry Review, Timber, Pilgrimage, Periódico de Poesía, Metrópolis, and more. Her poems are also featured in the Uruguayan women's section of Palabras Errantes, Plusamérica: Latin American Literature in Translation. Cesarco Eglin's poetry will appear in América invertida: An Anthology of Younger Uruguayan Poets forthcoming from the University of New Mexico Press in 2016. Cesarco Eglin's work has been twice nominated for a Pushcart Prize.

Tom Murphy's chapbook Horizon to Horizon was published in 2015 by Strike Syndicate. Recent work has been in 2016 Texas Poetry Calendar, Beatitude: Golden Anniversary Edition, Windward Review, Centrifuge, Nebula, Strike, Red River Review, Switchgrass Review and Voices de la Luna. Murphy has a poem forthcoming in each, The Great American Wise Ass Poetry Anthology and the Chupacabra Anthology. He lives with his wife and daughters and teaches at Texas A&M University—Corpus Christi.

Paul Toth is the author of four novels, his latest noted by USA Today as the 4th Best Independent Novel of 2011. His new release, The War Is Over, Let's Go Shopping, features his best short stories. He is also the founder and publisher of Eye Am Eye Books.

Alison Stone wrote Dangerous Enough, Borrowed Logic , From the Fool to the World, and They Sing at Midnight, which won the 2003 Many Mountains Moving Award. She was awarded Poetry's Frederick Bock Prize and New York Quarterly's Madeline Sadin award. She created The Stone Tarot and is a psychotherapist.

PW Covington has been active in the Texas Indie Lit scene for two decades. His full length book of poetry, Sacred Wounds, is published by Slough Press. He is a 100% service connected disabled veteran and a convicted felon.

Marcie Eanes is the author of "Cameo" a memoir detailing her life-threatening accident. She reinvented herself from newspaper reporter to traveling poet. Marcie is the author of two poetry collections "Sensual Sounds" and "Passion Zest." Marcie passed on September 14, 2015, she is published here posthumously and this work is dedicated to her poetry and her life.

Octavio Quintanilla is the author of the poetry collection, IF I GO MISSING (Slough Press, 2014. His work has appeared in Salamander, RHINO, Southwestern American Literature, Absurdo, and others. He teaches in the MA/MFA program at Our Lady of the Lake University.

Michael Aaron Casares lives in Austin, TX. He operates Virgogray Press, and edits Carcinogenic Poetry, an online poetry journal. His collection of poems, This Reality of Man, is available.

Steven Alvarez is Assistant Professor of Writing, Rhetoric, and Digital Studies at the University of Kentucky. He is the author of The Pocho Codex and The Xicano Genome, both published by Editorial Paroxismo. His chapbook Six Poems From the Codex Mojaodicus was the winner of the 2013 Rane Arroyo Poetry prize.

Kelly Talbot has edited books for 20 years, previously as an in-house editor for John Wiley and Sons Publishing, Macmillan Publishing, and Pearson Education, and now as the head of Kelly Talbot Editing

Services. His writing has appeared in dozens of magazines. He divides his time between Indianapolis, Indiana, and Timisoara, Romania.

Celina A. Gómez earned her MFA in Creative Writing and a graduate certificate in Mexican American Studies from the University of Texas – Pan American in 2015. She has been teaching high school English for eight years and coaches performance prose and poetry. She is the 2014 winner of the C.O.N.C.A Ultimate Poetry Boxing Championship. Currenlty, she lives in her hometown of Edinburg, Texas with her boyfriend, James, and their two dogs, Zero and Niki.

Abraham Peralta Vélez. Nacido en México, D.F. el 8 de julio de 1989. Licenciado en Letras Hispánicas por la UAM-I. Es director editorial de Tierra Húmeda, editorial de poesía. Fue fundador de la revista Hojas al aire. Ha publicado, a la fecha, dos libros de poesía Metamar y el marinero (2009) y Túrbido (2014). Ha colaborado en diversas presentaciones y revistas literarias.

Carlos Aguasaco Ph.D. (Bogotá, 1975).Profesor de Estudios Culturales en The City College of The City University of New York. Dirige The Americas Poetry festival of New York. Libros de poemas: Conversando con el Ángel (2003), Nocturnos del Caminante (2010), Antología de poetas hermafroditas (2014) & Poemas del metro de Nueva York (2014).

Edna Ochoa Poeta, narradora y dramaturga. Nació en la ciudad de México. Es autora de los poemarios Sombra para espejos y Respiración de raíces, del volumen de cuentos La cerca circular y de la novela Jirones de ayer. Sus obras han sido publicadas en diversas antologías: Escena con otra mirada, Antología de dramaturgas mexicanas, Teatro Joven de México, Obras de teatro para estudiantes de teatro, El Mundo Zurdo, La mujer rota, A través de la piel, y en revistas como Archipiélago, Ventana Abierta, Lucero, Hispanorama, BorderSenses, Camino Real y Grafemas. Ha traducido al español Zoot Suit de Luis Valdez y How the Frog and His Friend Saved Humanity de Víctor Villaseñor.

Mariano Morales is a writer, editor, translator and entrepreneur. He was born and raised in Monterrey, Mexico and migrated to the US in the pursuit of his professional studies. He is a member of the Board of the Latin American Foundation for the Arts. He has been invited

to several poetry festivals and events in Mexico and Texas. He is working in his second novel "Vaivén" and co-organizes the first Latin American International Poetry Festival. Mariano has a special academic interest in Mathematics and Technical Communication.

Iliana Hernández Partida, nació en Tepic, Nayarit. Vive en Ensenada B. C., México es Licenciada en Traducción y Perito Traductor. Colabora con artículos sobre arte y literatura en los suplementos culturales de los periódicos El Vigía, El Mexicano y en el medio electrónico Radar Político. Estudia la Maestría en Cultura Escrita en el Centro de Posgrado Sor Juana en la ciudad de Tijuana B. C.

Javier Gutiérrez Lozano (Puebla, México. 1988). Poeta, traductor y periodista. Director Editorial de Alcorce Ediciones. Editor de Revista Reflejo en Belgrado, Serbia, profesor de Literatura Contemporánea, y fundador del Concurso de Poesía D'Amicis. Recibió la Beca del Ministerio de Educación de la República de Serbia para realizar estudios especializados en política y cultura de los Balcanes. Sus textos han sido traducidos al idioma inglés, griego, rumano, bosnio, croata y serbio. Autor de los poemarios La magnitud de la distancia (México, 2014) y Vuelta al origen y otros poemas (Venezuela, 2014).

Javier Tinajero Rodríguez, @nuberrante, nació el 19 de marzo de 1982 en la Ciudad de México. Es autor de Párpados y pájaros (Amarcafé, México 2014). Estudió Artes Plásticas en el Cedart Luis Spota y posteriormente Filosofía en la Universidad del Claustro de Sor Juana. Es practicante de budismo desde 1998. Ha publicado poesía en distintas revistas nacionales e internacionales. Desde el año 2003 es el Coordinador de publicidad y diseño gráfico de Casa Tíbet México, y desde 2012 es el Director Creativo de la revista 84Mil, Palabras que despiertan. Actualmente dirige junto con Eduardo Medina y Julio Medellin la revista de literatura divergente y rizomática: Absurdo. Juan Nazario Soto Minero, campesino, bracero, trotamundos, maestro rural en Michoacán, escritor, narrador y poeta anarquista y autodidacta, Nacido hace más de 60 años en el pueblo de Tlalpujahua Michoacán, Ha viajado por toda la República Mexicana, documentando en carne propia la lucha valerosa de su pueblo por la liberación definitiva. Autor de la novela antipoliciaca HOMÖNIMO y del libro de poemas, ensayos y entrevistas TEXTOS DE COMBATE, más otro poemario en preparación. Ideólogo del colectivo La Decena Trágica.

Nephtalí De León is a former migrant worker that became a Poet/ Painter/Playwright. Without a formal education he is known for his lively poetry, and his illustrated writings for children as well as for adults. Most of his works are bilingual and tri-cultural. In 2012 alone he had 3 books published in Spain, (one by the University of Valencia) while his poetry has been translated into Chinese, Arabic, Russian, Catalán, and other languages.

Pilar Rodríguez Aranda (Mexico City, 1961) is a writer, translator and video artist. Her poetry has been included in many magazines and anthologies; she published her first collection of poetry, Asunto de mujeres (Cascada de Palabras Cartonera) in 2012, and in 2014, the plaquette, Verdes Lazos (Rio Arriba). She is 100 Thousand Poets for Change coordinator in Mexico and member of "Writing for Peace" Advisory Panel. http://pilarpoeta.blogspot.com

Takeshi Edmundo López. (México D.F., 1984), poeta, articulista. Ganó el segundo lugar en el concurso de poesía del Día Internacional del Libro 2006 donde los poemas ganadores se publicaron en la Gaceta Acatlán, UNAM, con un tiraje de 15,000 unidades. Ha publicado en revistas como Primera dama, La Peste, Efecto Pigmalión, Radiador Magazine, Los bastardos de la uva, El Humo, Anomalía, entre otras, colaborador en distintos blogs (Juntaversos, Ágape de luces). Incluido en la antología digital Pájaros negros (Colombia, 2012). En la antología Árbol en llamas (Sediento ediciones, 2013). En la antología Poetas del tercero milenio volumen bilingüe Italiano-español (Lo spazio internacional art & literature editions, Fondi, Italia. 2014).

Ulises Paniagua Narrador, poeta, videasta y dramaturgo. Ha publicado tres poemarios: Del amor y otras miserias (Fridaura, 2009), Guardián de las Horas (Eterno femenino, 2012), y Nocturno imperio de los proscritos (Sediento Ediciones, 2014, Enciclopedia de las Letras Mexicanas, INBA, CONACULTA-FLM); y tres libros de cuentos Patibulario, cuentos al final del túnel, (Mutibilda, 2011), Nadie duerme esta noche (Fridaura, 2012), e Historias de la ruina (Sediento Ediciones, 2013, Enciclopedia de las Letras Mexicanas, INBA, CONACULTA-FLM); así como los CDs sonoro-poéticos Cuadriversiones y Clandestinos y nocturnos (Colectivo Pena Ajena, 2013 y 2014).

Vanessa Torres Poeta y Antropóloga (Bogotá, Colombia 1978) Egresada de la escuela de Antropología de La Universidad Nacional de Colombia, ha combinado la labor poética y de ensayo con la investigación antropológica. Obsesionada con las imágenes y la necesidad del reconocimiento del valor político de los actos creativos ha hecho publicaciones y colaboraciones para magazines de opinión y literarios como la Revista Literaria Calle Ficción del periódico Debate Press España junto con el escritor Venezolano Edgar Borges y el escritor y artista Sevillano Juan Manuel Álvarez.

Gerald Padilla. Educator and translator. Co-Author of the trilingual childrens book Animales de mi Tierra/Animals of my land/ Noyolcanyolqueh.

Xánath Caraza is a traveler, educator, poet and short story writer. Her book of poetry, Sílabas de viento / Syllables of Wind, received the 2015 International Book Award for Poetry. It also received Honorable Mention for Best Book of Poetry in Spanish in the 2015 International Latino Book Awards. She is the recipient of the Beca Nebrija para Creadores 2014 from the Instituto Franklin in Spain. Her book Conjuro was awarded second place in the 'Best Poetry Book in Spanish' category and received honorable mention in the 'Best First Book in Spanish, Mariposa Award' category of the 2013 International Latino Book Awards. She was named number one of the 2013 Top Ten "New" Latino Authors to Watch (and Read) by LatinoStories.com.

Antonella Barina ha publicado, entre otros: Nessun Alibi (con anna Lombardo), Turning. Le città della luna, Margheramondo selezione poetica, Aria. Il prezzo della poesia.

Silvia Favaretto ha publicado, entre otros: La carne del tiempo, Parole d'acqua, Giardino ardente, La noche de los cuerpos, Desde la mirilla del ombligo, Quiero tanto a Julio, Speleologia della pietra della follia.

Lucia Guidorizzi ha publicado, entre otros: Confini , Scandalose entropie. Riflessioni poetiche sugli abusi prodotti dal divenire storico, Ibrida Hybris , Quadrilunio. Una tetralogia dell'Anima, Milagros , Nel paese dei castelli di sabbia, Controcanto.

Cinzia Marulli ha publicado, entre otros: Agave, Las mantas de Dios, Percezioni dell'invisibile

Anita Menegozzo ha publicado, entre otros: Sordo senza rimedio è chi non vuol sentire, La goccia di me stessa con cui scrivo.

Giorgia Pollastri ha publicado, entre otros: Rime filastrocche e poesie, Piume, Ciclo-Kiklos

Mina Gligorić nacío en Belgrado el 1989. Su mayor placer es caminar por la Facultad de Filología en Universidad de Belgrado, en la cual estudia literatura y lucha por salvar la literatura y la lengua serbia del olvido. Habla inglés y español. Su poesía está publicada en muchas revistas literarias Serbias: Gaceta Literaria, Diario poético, Revista literaria, Los Techos, El desarollo. Ha publicado un libro de poesía La manzana de Adán (2012). Ha actuado en los Festivales Internacionales de Poesía en Belgrado, Serbia 2011, en Coyoacán, Cuidad de México 2014 y en Granada.

Miriam Damaris Maldonado Nació en Noviembre 21 de 1981, en Puerto Rico. Estudios en Psicologia, Trabajo Social y Género. Activista, Feminista, Escritora y Poetisa. Coolaboradora y creadora en el 1er y 2ndo Festival Internacional de Poesia Grito de Mujer; Houston 2013 y 2014. Ganó el Festival Literario 2009 de la Universidad Interamericana de Puerto Rico con el género poesía. Sus escritos han sido publicados en los principales periódicos de su pais, así como en el periodico Feminista Voz de Voces.

Ken Jones is a poet and musician who has published numerous projects in both genres worldwide. His latest full band CD KEEPING UP WITH THE JONES by POETKEN AND FRIENDS is available on all digital platforms.

Ed O'Casey received his MA from the University of North Texas and his MFA from New Mexico State University. He teaches full time at Nicolet Area Technical College in northern Wisconsin, where he is currently learning how to avoid freezing to death in his own living room. His poems have appeared or are upcoming in Berkeley Poetry Review, Cold Mountain Review, Tulane Review, Oak Bend Review, Euphony, Poetry Quarterly, NANO Fiction, and West Trade Review.

Jessica Helen Lopez is the current City of Albuquerque Poet Laureate and the Poet-In-Residence for the Albuquerque Museum of Art and History. She has also been a featured writer for 30 Poets in their 30's by MUZZLE magazine. Lopez is a nationally recognized award-winning slam poet, and holds the title of 2012 and 2014 Women of the World City of ABQ Champion. She is a member of the Macondo Foundation. Founded by Sandra Cisneros, it is an association of socially engaged writers united to advance creativity, foster generosity, and... honor community. Her first collection of poetry, Always Messing With Them Boys (West End Press, 2011) made the Southwest Book of the Year reading list and was also awarded the Zia Book Award presented by NM Women Press. Her second collection of poetry, Cunt. Bomb. is published by Swimming with Elephants Publication (2014). Her third collection, The Language of Bleeding: Poems for the International Poetry Festival, Nicaragua (SWEP) is a limited release in honor of her ambassadorial visit to Granada, Nicaragua.

Corina Carmona is a Chicana feminist artist and an art education graduate student who has a mural on the wall of the Whole Woman's Health clinic in the Rio Grande Valley where upwards of 1.3 million live. The clinic is the only one south of San Antonio that offers abortions. Her artwork has appeared on several bookcovers and she is a public high school teacher.

The Editors

Rossy Evelin Lima is a linguist and translator. Her fist poetry book
Ecos de Barro published by Otras Voces Press was recognized by the
International Latino Book Awards 2014. She received the Gabriela
Mistral Award 2010 by the National Hispanic Honor Society. She was
awarded the international poetry award Concorso di poesia Altino
in Italy. The author has been published in numerous anthologies
and literary magazines in Spain, Canada, USA, Argentina, Chile,
Venezuela, Italy and Mexico. She was included in the Antología
de Poesía y Narrativa Hispanoamericana (2015 Madrid, Spain). Her
second book of poetry Augacamino/Waterpath will be published by
Mouthfeel Press. Lima co-organizes the Sin Fronteras Independent
Book Fest.

Christopher Carmona was the inaugural writer-in-residence for
the Langdon Review Writers Residency Program in 2015. His story,
"Strange Leaves," was the third finalist in the Texas Observer Short
Story Contest of 2014. He was also a Pushcart Prize nominee in 2013
and a nominee for the Alfredo Cisneros de Miral Foundation Award
for Writers in 2011. He has been published in numerous journals and
magazines including Trickster Literary Journal, Interstice, vandal.,
Bordersenses, & the Sagebrush Review. His first collection of short
stories entitled, The Road to Llorona Park is to be published by
Stephen F. Austin University Press in 2016. He was a co-editor for The
Beatest State In The Union: An Anthology of Beat Texas Writing
published by Lamar University Press. He was also co-writer for a
scholarly conversation book entitled Nuev@s Voces Poeticas: A
Dialogue about New Chican@ Identities and he has two collections
of poetry: beat and I Have Always Been Here. Finally, he is the
organizer of the Annual Beat Poetry and Arts Festival and the Artistic
Director of the Coalition of New Chican@ Artists.

www.ingramcontent.com/pod-product-compliance
Lightning Source LLC
Chambersburg PA
CBHW050510260626
47157CB00004B/1272